THE
TEAM CAPTAIN'S
LEADERSHIP MANUAL

ADDITIONAL RESOURCES BY JEFF JANSSEN

Books

The Team Captain's Culture Manual: The Complete Guide to Working with Your Team Leaders to Build a Championship Culture

How to Build and Sustain a Championship Culture

Championship Team Building: What Every Coach Needs to Know to Build a Motivated, Committed, and Cohesive Team

Jeff Janssen's Peak Performance Playbook: 50 Drills, Activities & Ideas to Inspire Your Team, Build Mental Toughness & Improve Team Chemistry

The Seven Secrets of Successful Coaches: How to Unlock and Unleash Your Team's Full Potential

The Mental Makings of Champions: How to Win The Mental Game

How to Develop Relentless Competitors

Develop Relentless Competitors Drillbook

The Commitment Continuum™ System

Websites

Team Captains Network—www.TeamCaptainsNetwork.com
Championship Coaches Network—www.ChampionshipCoachesNetwork.com

Visit www.janssensportsleadership.com or call 1-888-721-TEAM

THE
TEAM CAPTAIN'S
LEADERSHIP MANUAL

The Complete Guide to Developing
Team Leaders Whom Coaches Respect
and Teammates Trust

JEFF JANSSEN, M.S.

Winning The Mental Game
Cary, North Carolina

Substantial discounts on bulk quantities of this book are available to athletic departments, coaches' associations, and other organizations. For details and discount information, please call 1-888-721-TEAM.

Published by Winning The Mental Game
6841 Piershill Lane, Cary, NC 27519
Phone: 1-888-721-TEAM
Fax: (919) 303-4338
Email: jeff@jeffjanssen.com
Website: www.jeffjanssen.com

The Paradoxical Commandments are printed with the permission of the author. (c) Copyright Kent M. Keith 1968, renewed 2001. www.paradoxicalcommandments.com.

Publisher's Cataloging-in-Publication
(*Provided by Quality Books, Inc.*)

Janssen, Jeff.
    The team captain's leadership manual : the complete guide to developing team leaders whom coaches respect and teammates trust / Jeff Janssen.
        p. cm.
        Includes bibliographic references and index.
        Audience: 13-24 years.
        LCCN 2003108606
        ISBN 1-892882-11-6

    1. Teamwork (Sports) 2. Leadership.   I. Title

GV706.8.J36 2003   796'.01
                    QBI03-200532

Printed in the United States of America
10 9 8 7 6

DEDICATION

To my mom—Mary Janssen

Thanks for being such a great role model for me as a mother, school board president, and community activist. You have taught me that being a leader means setting high standards, caring about people, and putting others first. Thanks for always believing in me, challenging me, and encouraging me. I hope that this manual teaches many leaders the principles you emphasized like "When good does nothing, evil triumphs." Know that your legacy of leadership will be carried on by the readers of this book and make a difference in the lives of many for generations to come.

With Greatest Admiration and Love, Your Son,
Jeffrey John

SPORTS LEADERSHIP DEVELOPMENT SERIES

Our popular Sports Leadership Development Series provides athletes, coaches, and athletic administrators with a practical, progressive, and proven sports leadership development training program that spans a student-athlete's entire career. The comprehensive curriculum targets student-athletes at their specific level of leadership development. The series starts with teaching the critical self leadership skills of responsibility, accountability, and commitment and then progresses on to the more advanced skills of effective team leadership and building a championship culture. So no matter where your athletes might be in terms of their personal leadership development, you'll have the appropriate level of training for them.

Level 1: Personal Responsibility—The Athlete's Responsibility Manual

The Athlete's Responsibility Manual trains student-athletes how to take full responsibility for themselves by owning their choices, decisions, and actions. The six-module program is geared for all freshmen to complete as early as possible during their first year - or as a great summer read before they start school.

Level 2: Team Accountability—The Athlete's Accountability Manual (Coming Fall of 2017)

The Athlete's Accountability Manual shows athletes how their attitudes and actions significantly impact their teammates' and coaches' success and failure. This six-module program extends and expands on the material in Level 1 and can be done with all freshmen in the first semester of their first year.

Level 3: Commitment—The Athlete's Commitment Manual

The Athlete's Commitment Manual trains student-athletes how to completely commit to their task, training, and team through the use of the powerful Commitment Continuum™ tool. This six-module program can be done with all freshmen in the second semester of their first year.

Level 4: Team Leadership—The Team Captain's Leadership Manual

Designed for emerging team leaders, *The Team Captain's Leadership Manual* is a 10-module leadership development program that trains student-athletes how to be effective Leaders by Example and Vocal Leaders. Use it early on with your sophomores who demonstrate leadership potential.

Level 5: Championship Culture—The Team Captain's Culture Manual

Designed for established team leaders, *The Team Captain's Culture Manual* teaches captains how to best partner with the coaches to build and sustain a Championship Culture in your program. Use this 10-module, advanced leadership development program with your junior and senior team captains.

For more info on the Sports Leadership Development Series visit
www.JanssenSportsLeadership.com

ACKNOWLEDGMENTS

LEADERS CANNOT BE SUCCESSFUL WITHOUT A DEDICATED TEAM. I was fortunate to have a great team of people who did a lot of behind the scenes work to help me write, edit, and refine this manual. It is my pleasure to acknowledge them here.

First, a very sincere thank you to all of the captains and coaches who I have been privileged to work with and learn from over the last decade. I hope I might have taught you half as much as you have taught me. I appreciate your trust, honesty, and respect.

Special thanks to everyone who read drafts of the manual and contributed their insights: Becky Ahlgren, Kimberley Amirault, Ryan Bachur, Gary Barnett, Becky Bell, Jane Bennett, Greg Dale, Liz Eitzen, Aaron Eldred, Francis Forgues, Matt Forgues, Brenda Frese, Stephanie Glance, Gail Goestenkors, Lizz Greene, Bob Harmison, Kaila Holtz, Carol Hutchins, Kristi Janssen, Thad Leffingwell, Bart Lerner, Jill McCartney, Don Meyer, Patrick Murphy, Terry Pettit, Ken Ravizza, Tammy Shain, Greg Shelley, Pat Summitt, Marge Willadsen, Ward Wittman, Wes Worrell, and Kay Yow. Thanks for sharing your wisdom with me and the readers of this manual.

Thank you to Jennifer Brinegar, Mindy Claggett, Beth Feickert, Doug Finch, Larry Gallo, Patrick Gleason, Jeff Hull, Jon Jackson, Debby Jennings, Dave Lohse, Chenelle Miller, Joe Moore, Chad Onken, Cindy Peters, Dave Plati, Anna Schmidt, LeeAnne Sears, Wendi Seiler, Lance Taylor, Janice Theurer, Bill Turnage, and Wes Worrell for their assistance in contributing pictures to the manual. Thank you to Tony and Sherry Roberts of The Roberts Group for their graphic design expertise and the good people at Data Reproductions. It is fun and comforting to work with true professionals.

Most of all, thanks to my highly supportive family. Ryan and Jill—thank you for your patience while Daddy was working on the computer. You continually remind me that my most important leadership responsibility is being your father. Help me practice the principles I preach in this manual. I know that you both will become leaders who make a real difference. You are children of destiny; you are destined for great things!

Kristi, once again I could not do this without you. This was truly a collaborative effort. I appreciate your insights and ideas on all aspects of this manual. You are blessed with a sharp mind and caring heart—two of the qualities I love most about you. Thanks for telling me what I need to hear even when I am partial to my ideas. Your encouragement, support, and love mean the world to me.

Finally, I am thrilled to have the opportunity to dedicate this book to my mother. Mom, thank you for always planting seeds of success in my mind and challenging me to be a leader. You always told me, "You are a child of destiny; You are destined for great things." I hope this manual is part of what you meant. May it make as big of a difference in others' lives as you have in mine and Jaclyn's.

TABLE OF CONTENTS

FOREWORD

YOU WON'T WIN CONSISTENTLY WITHOUT GOOD TEAM LEADERSHIP. It's just that plain and simple. You've got to have players who are willing to buy into your system, demand the best from themselves and their teammates, and hold their teammates accountable. Sure, I demand a lot from our players. But I demand even more from our leaders.

I rely on our leaders to set the tone for the season, handle discipline, keep me informed, and help our freshmen adjust. For example, we assign our upperclassmen mentoring roles with our incoming freshmen. We use a "buddy system" where the upperclassmen make sure the freshmen know their way around campus, get to class on time, eat well, etc. The upperclassmen check up on them frequently to see if they have any questions or problems. It's up to the leaders to make sure everyone is responsible and accountable.

We've been fortunate to have our share of effective leaders at Tennessee. I really think it's one of the keys to the long-term consistency of our program. These leaders have helped us get through some tough times as well as inspired and willed us to win even when the odds were stacked against us.

More than winning, I believe our job as coaches is to develop our players into responsible leaders. Sure we teach them how to be better athletes. But that's not all I want to be known for. I want the young women who come into our program to become better people and better leaders by the time they leave.

I am proud of our national championships. But I am more proud of the fact that over two dozen of our former players or staffers have become coaches at the collegiate and high school level. Over a dozen of them are head coaches. Our job as coaches is to develop responsible leaders in all walks of life: coaches, teachers, business managers, doctors, mothers, you name it. That to me is real success.

I have great admiration and respect for Jeff's work with coaches and student-athletes. His innovative ideas have made a difference in our program as well as many programs across the country. He has the unique ability to transform critical concepts like team building, mental toughness, and leadership into practical and easy to use strategies that can be implemented by coaches and athletes alike. Like his other books, *The Team Captain's Leadership Manual* provides coaches and captains with a proven system for developing responsible team leaders. Like myself, I'm sure you can't wait to use the ideas in this book to develop (and become) successful leaders who will make a difference in your sport and in life.

PAT SUMMITT
Head Women's Basketball Coach Emeritus
University of Tennessee
Eight-time National Champions

FOREWORD

ALONG WITH OUR WORLD-CLASS COACHES AT NORTH CAROLINA, I believe strong student-athlete leadership is an absolute must for building and maintaining a successful team and athletic department. In fact, we feel leadership is so critical to our athletic department's success both on and off the playing fields that we developed the nation's first comprehensive, ongoing Leadership Academy in collegiate athletics.

The Carolina Leadership Academy develops, challenges, and supports our student-athletes and coaches in their continual quest to become world-class leaders in athletics, academics, and life. Our goal has been to establish Carolina not only as a great school and successful athletics program, but as a national model for training and developing leadership skills.

The Carolina Leadership Academy has made a major impact on our athletic department. We've seen big benefits and continually get great feedback from our student-athletes and coaches. I wholeheartedly agree with Anson Dorrance, our women's soccer coach and one of the most successful collegiate coaches ever, when he says, "The Carolina Leadership Academy is one of the finest things our athletic department has done in the over thirty years I have been here. I can clearly see the program's impact on and off the field."

While we are certainly proud of our athletic and academic accomplishments, we especially value the long-term effects that the Carolina Leadership Academy will have as our students graduate and take their leadership skills out into the world.

With *The Team Captain's Leadership Manual,* Jeff Janssen provides you with the foundational concepts we use to develop our student-athlete leaders at Carolina. His book is an excellent resource for student-athletes as well as for coaches and athletic administrators who want to develop strong leaders. It is my honor and privilege to recommend it to you. Based on our experience at Carolina, I assure you it will make a difference.

DICK BADDOUR
Director of Athletics Emeritus
University of North Carolina

Note to Athletes: This Introduction is specifically written for your coach so feel free to skip over this section. Please turn to page xxxi for the Athlete's Introduction.

Welcome to *The Team Captain's Leadership Manual: The Complete Guide to Developing Team Leaders Whom Coaches Respect and Teammates Trust.* This one-of-a-kind manual is designed to help you develop the responsible and respected team captains and leaders you need to be successful. Of course your leadership as a coach is critical—that goes without saying. But to be successful, you also must have at least one athlete, if not a few, who can effectively lead their fellow teammates. You must have both Leaders by Example and Vocal Leaders who are bought in to your system, reinforce what you do, hold their teammates accountable to a higher standard, and watch your back by diffusing difficulties, conflicts, and problems—or at least making you aware of them. Without effective team captains and responsible team leaders, you are likely in for a very long and frustrating season.

The Importance of Effective Team Leaders

Here's what some of your coaching colleagues have said about the importance of having effective team leaders.

"Talent is important. But the single most important ingredient after you get the talent is internal leadership. It's not the coaches as much as one single person or people on the team who set higher standards than that team would normally set for itself. I really believe that that's been ultimately important for us."
MIKE KRZYZEWSKI, DUKE MEN'S BASKETBALL COACH

"Talent will get you about seven or eight wins. Discipline will start pushing that to nine. Then when you get leadership that's when the magic starts happening. It's when you start getting rings and some really cool things are happening to your team."
URBAN MEYER, OHIO STATE FOOTBALL COACH

"Teams that have strong leadership have a decided advantage. If you look at the great NBA teams of the past 15 years, one of the common threads is they all had great veteran leaders . . . Each had his own style but they all demanded excellence from the people around them. Not just once in a while, not just when things were going well for them, but all the time."
RICK PITINO, LOUISVILLE MEN'S BASKETBALL COACH

*"Having great leadership is a big key to success.
It's really the leaders' team because they are the ones whom the rest of the players, especially the freshmen, look up to when setting the standards. Our team will go as far as our leaders are willing to take us."*
MIKE CANDREA, ARIZONA SOFTBALL COACH
USA SOFTBALL OLYMPIC HEAD COACH

"The key to being successful is to have great leadership on your team. It takes a lot of maturity and a lot of players who are interested in the welfare of the team, who are willing to try and influence and inspire other players on the team to help everybody do what they need to do."
NICK SABAN, ALABAMA FOOTBALL COACH

"Because I understand how important leaders are to the success of the team, I've worked hard at selecting the captains and helping them develop the leadership qualities that I feel are important."
JERRY YEAGLEY, LEGENDARY INDIANA MEN'S SOCCER COACH

As you can see, many of sport's most successful and respected coaches readily admit that a big key to their success depends largely on the quality of leaders they have within the team. You too understand that effective leaders are not a luxury but a vital necessity. Your captains are the heart and soul of your team.

Good Team Leaders Are an Extension of You

Most coaches talk about needing team leaders who are an extension of themselves. To be successful, you must have someone who knows your philosophy and understands your game plan—and can communicate and reinforce it to the rest of the team. You need someone who can keep your team focused during the heat of competition when you are on the sidelines. You need someone to be your voice in the locker room. And you need a respected leader who can hold their teammates accountable during the many times outside of practice when you can't be around.

Effective Team Leaders Impact Your Success, Sanity, Satisfaction and Significance

Effective team leaders impact the most important areas you hold near and dear as a coach: your success, sanity, satisfaction and significance.

Your Success

As you reflect on some of your most successful seasons, I'll bet that more often than not you had at least one if not a couple of leaders who set the tone for the rest of the team. And conversely, you probably had mediocre, poor, or non-existent leadership during most, if not all of your most disappointing seasons.

Team leaders have a big bearing on your team's success. Why? Because successful leaders dictate so many of the important intangible factors that influence winning. In essence, an effective leader is the linchpin of your team. Your other athletes will rise or fall to the level of your team leader. The quality of your team's leadership dictates the rest of your athletes' work ethic, attitude, focus, confidence, mental toughness, team chemistry, and virtually all other aspects of your program.

Your Sanity

Aside from success, quality team leaders, or the lack thereof, also greatly influence your sanity. Effective team leaders proactively prevent a lot of the problems that frustrate you, give you gray hair or cause it to fall out, keep you up at night, and drive many good coaches right out of coaching. They can minimize team conflicts, positively police your players in the community, and help your athletes (and parents) understand and accept their roles.

Your Satisfaction and Significance

Finally, developing effective team leaders provides you with a tremendous sense of satisfaction which transcends winning. Sure you want to win. But you also want to teach your athletes skills that will help them become winners in the game of life. Developing and mentoring the athletes on your team into leaders is one of the most important and rewarding aspects of coaching. You have the power and the privilege to teach your athletes skills that will impact them for the rest of their lives. Keep in mind that the athletes you have today are the doctors, lawyers, mayors, managers, teachers, coaches, and parents of tomorrow.

Ultimately your true significance as a coach will not be measured in how many goals, touchdowns, runs, or points your athletes score. Your leadership as a coach will be measured in your ability to develop better people. Herein lies your real significance as a coach.

"If the only reason I coached was to win college basketball games, my life would be pretty shallow. I coach not only because I love it, but because I have the chance to teach and interact with young people."

MIKE KRZYZEWSKI, DUKE MEN'S BASKETBALL

"If you plan for one year, plant rice. If you plan for 10 years, plant a tree. If you plan for 100 years, educate a child."

CHINESE PROVERB

Effective Team Leaders . . .

Investing the time to develop effective team leaders will pay off in a multitude of ways for you and your team. Here are the primary benefits effective leaders will bring to your team:

1. Ensure High Standards and a Strong Work Ethic

Without effective team leaders, mediocrity is the goal of the team. The team motto becomes "Do just enough to get by" and "That's good enough." No one steps up and sets the tone for the rest of the team to follow. Further, when some athletes inevitably slack off and cut corners, no one is willing to constructively confront them on it and let them know that their laziness is unacceptable and detrimental to the team.

Great team leaders set and maintain the standards for everyone else to follow. They consistently give it their all and demand that their teammates do the same. This is especially important when you have freshmen and other newcomers joining the team on a regular basis. The newcomers often look to their veteran teammates to determine the standards of the team. If the leaders are slacking off and cutting corners, it is very easy for the rookies to do the same.

2. Keep Your Team from Crumbling Under Pressure and Adversity

Without a team leader, teams often crumble under pressure and adversity. Athletes quickly get frustrated with opponents, officials, teammates, and themselves and lose their composure. They get distracted by their past mistakes and worry about making future errors. Further, when teams fall apart they tend to blame each other which distracts, divides, and destroys your team. Without a team leader, your athletes isolate themselves from the team instead of pulling together and staying tough. This lack of leadership and mental toughness during adversity often forces you to burn precious time-outs and make unwanted substitutions during the game. Worse, your team ends up beating itself because they self-destruct rather than staying tough and forcing your opponents to beat you. You can likely trace many of your losses back to the lack of ineffective team leaders.

Effective team leaders help their teammates weather the inevitable storms of adversity that occur during games and throughout the season. When adversity strikes, great leaders maintain their own composure which keeps their teammates under control. They then can refocus the team back on the task at hand. Good team leaders are a calming force who are able to help their teammates adjust and refocus.

3. Build Better Team Chemistry

Effective team leaders promote a positive sense of team chemistry. They welcome and take the new members of your team under their wing so the younger players feel accepted and have someone to turn to should something go wrong—as often is the case for freshmen. Effective team leaders prevent cliques from developing as they look to break down barriers, unify their teammates, and rally them around a common goal.

4. Help You Take the Pulse of the Team

If you don't have a good leader you can trust, you might miss some important things happening with your athletes and team. You might not know why a certain player all of a sudden isn't playing well or why another might not be communicating with you any more. Further, it might seem like you have lost your players' enthusiasm but you aren't sure why.

Effective team leaders help keep you connected to your team. They keep you informed about how players might be doing, who is struggling, and if there is any dissension brewing amongst the team. Not only do great team leaders keep you up to date on the pulse of the team, they can also provide you with input on changes you might be contemplating or ones you have already instituted.

5. Minimize and Manage Conflict

Additionally, good team leaders will help you manage the inevitable conflict that occurs on every team between athletes, coaches, parents, and others. They can help their teammates better understand why they are getting limited playing time, thus preventing them from running to their parents and having them call you to complain about it. They can often handle and even solve a lot of problems before you even have to get involved. This frees up your time to focus on what you do best—coaching. Good leaders then make your job easier as a coach by preventing, minimizing, and handling a significant portion of the typical problems that beset teams, so you don't have to.

6. Help You Sign and Screen Recruits

In college, your team leaders will often serve as hosts for potential recruits. The captains go a long way in helping recruits feel comfortable with your program and feel a sense of acceptance and family with the current team members. Your captains can sell the benefits of your program, handle any of the recruit's concerns and objections, get a feel for how the recruit might be leaning, and provide insights into the recruit's character. There have been instances where captains have clued in coaches to potential red flags on a recruiting trip that coaches may not have seen in the recruiting process. Effective team captains will help you sign the right people for your program and screen those who could end up being more trouble than they are worth.

7. Are Your Best Insurance Against Stupidity

Finally, good leaders are your best insurance policy against your athletes making stupid decisions on campus and in the community that could tarnish you and your program. Good leaders will help you control and curb the common teenage and young adult temptations like drinking, drugs, sex, hazing, gambling, and the myriad of other problems that often end up as the talk of the town or embarrassing headlines in the local and even national media. Minimizing these problems alone will provide you with many more restful evenings.

This positive policing role is especially important because as a coach you can only be with your athletes so many hours of the day. Obviously you get to spend time with them at practice, but the rest of the day they have a variety of choices which you cannot constantly watch and monitor, nor should you want or have to. However, great team leaders tend to be around their teammates more and can be a positive influence on them. This is especially true on weekend evenings when athletes can be tempted to do things that could potentially have negative effects on themselves and the team, not to mention your program's reputation. Great team leaders look out for their teammates and are willing to constructively confront them when necessary.

Investing in Leadership Skills

Because they understand the many benefits that effective leaders bring, many professional teams are now investing millions of dollars in aging players who are past their prime. Although their physical skills have diminished, coaches and upper management sign these older players primarily because of their veteran leadership skills. They want someone who can teach the rookies what it means to be a professional. They need someone whom the young players will look up to, and most of all, listen to. They need someone who can put the team first and is focused on winning, instead of focusing on the next big contract or endorsement deal. Many professional teams are willing to pay millions of dollars not necessarily for great talent, but for solid and respected leadership. As a college or high school coach, you obviously don't need to invest the money. But you must invest the time necessary to find, develop, and retain effective team leaders.

Why the Glaring Lack of Leaders in Today's Athletes?

Unfortunately, more and more coaches bemoan the problem that today's athletes seem to lack the leadership skills compared to those of the past. They say that it's so difficult to find good leaders anymore. Why is leadership so tough to find in today's athletes?

While there are a variety of plausible explanations, many of my colleagues believe that the lack of leadership skills can actually be traced to the growth and explosion of adult-run youth sports programs. Ironically, the organized sports opportunities that so many parents have created for their children are actually working against their children's development of leadership skills. In the past, when kids were left up to themselves to play sports on their own, they were forced to develop leadership skills. The kids picked the teams, decided the rules, determined the lineup, officiated their own games, handled conflicts and difficulties, etc. All of these responsibilities required kids to develop leadership skills. Now, children get so few opportunities to play on their own because everything is so adult-organized and controlled. With fewer opportunities to lead, there are going to be fewer leaders.

From Whom Much Is Expected, Little Is Taught

So much is expected of team captains and leaders. The problem is that so few of them are ever formally taught the leadership skills they need to do the job effectively. Expecting your athletes to be great leaders without investing the time to teach, coach, and develop their leadership skills is like expecting them to speak fluid Swahili when they have never even heard the language. Virtually all captains want to be effective leaders—you just need to provide them with the necessary insights and skills to do so. Like physical skills, leadership skills must be systematically taught, developed, and practiced if you want to see them used and mastered by your athletes.

That's what *The Team Captain's Leadership Manual* is all about. This com-prehensive leadership program is designed to help you teach your current and prospective leaders the insights, strategies, and skills they will need to be effective leaders for you and your team. It is also designed to provide you with a practical and proven system for identifying, educating, and developing your leaders over time. Rome wasn't built in a day and neither are effective team leaders.

You Need to Be Involved in This 10-Week Program

To be maximally effective, I strongly encourage you to get actively and closely involved in the leadership development process. Sure you could hand your lead-ers this manual, tell them to read it, and hold them accountable for it. But like developing physical skills, developing effective leaders requires your ongoing feedback, coaching, questions, discussion, and insights. If you want to develop the kind of leaders your program needs to be successful, you must mentor and mold them to meet your needs and expectations. If you want your leaders to be extensions of you, you must extend yourself to them.

That's why I strongly encourage you to go through *The Team Captain's Leadership Manual* right along with your athletes. The manual is divided into

10 manageable yet detailed chapters which cover the essential components of leadership. I suggest that you and your athletes make a firm commitment to this 10-week leadership development program. You'll independently read a chapter a week over the next 10 weeks—preferably before practices start, at the very beginning of your season, or during your off season. Ideally, it is best to have as much of the material covered as realistically possible before you begin your competitive season.

Just as your athletes are doing, read the chapters, take notes, answer the questions, complete the exercises, and jot down any comments and questions you might have as you work through the material. Because learning is an active process, I have also included some practical exercises for you and your athletes at the end of each chapter. These activities are designed to provide your team leaders with a variety of viewpoints on the topic of leadership—plus help them develop important insights and relationships with other leaders in your area. I encourage you to have your captains complete these exercises whenever possible. If you have more than one athlete going through the manual with you, you may want to assign each athlete a different exercise if you are pressed for time.

Designate a specific 30 to 60 minute time frame each week where you and your leader(s) will get together to discuss the chapter you completed for the week. I've included a Coach/Captain Meeting Notes page at the end of each chapter for you and your captains to jot down ideas and goals from your discussions. Not only will weekly meetings provide you and your leaders the opportunity to work through the manual, practice the strategies, and absorb the material over time, but it will also give you the opportunity to communicate regularly, understand each other better, monitor the team, and develop and strengthen the trust between you. To be an effective extension of you, your leaders must know exactly how you think and what you want for them to be successful.

Investing the time to work on the manual with your leaders clearly demonstrates to them how important you consider their role to be. Being an effective team leader is an extremely demanding and difficult challenge for many of them—especially as a teenager or young adult facing tremendous peer pressure. They will need your support and guidance throughout the season. They need to know that you believe in them and trust them. The regular meetings will give you the opportunity to demonstrate your commitment to and concern for them.

Once you have completed the 10 chapters with your athletes, I still encourage you to meet regularly throughout the season. As you will see, I have included a Captain's Weekly Monitoring Sheet in the final Summary chapter for your leaders to use during the season. This sheet will help you and your leaders stay tuned to the vital signs of your team as you look to proactively set your team up for success as well as address any concerns or problems which might arise. Continual communication and listening will be key throughout the season.

How to Identify and Select Your Team Leaders

Of course, before you begin the program, you must identify who your actual and potential leaders might be. Because team leaders are so important, you must take careful consideration in selecting and developing these people. In an ideal world, your best player would also be your best leader. When this is the case, take advantage of it because your athletes will respect your captain's talent and leadership skills. More often than not however, your leader will not be the most talented person on your team—yet their contribution to your team's success will be just as valuable, if not more so.

What is the best way to select your team captains? There are a variety of methods that coaches use to determine their team leaders—each of them with associated pros and cons. While you probably already have a preferred selection method that works for you, take a minute to look over the variety of options you have in determining your team leaders.

1. Coach chooses captains.

Obviously, when you choose your own captains, you get to select the people who you feel comfortable working with and believe will do the best job. While this option works well for you, you risk choosing someone who is not as respected or trusted by their teammates. Further you take the awesome power of involvement away from your team by showing them that you do not value their input. In a survey I conducted of college and high school coaches, I discovered that 25% of coaches use this option to determine their team captains.

2. Players vote for captains.

A second option is to let your players vote for captains. This has the benefit of showing your players that you respect them enough to allow them to determine the team captains. Further, they will likely choose the people they respect. However, I suggest you remind them on the front end that this is not a popularity contest. Invest the time before the vote to clarify the specific characteristics and skills necessary to be an effective captain (see pages 13–14). Your athletes should then vote for the people whom they respect and who they feel can effectively lead the team. The possible drawback is that your team might pick someone you dislike or do not think would be an effective captain. This option was used by 34% of the coaches surveyed.

3. Athletes nominate/coach makes final decision.

A hybrid of the first two, this option gives you the best of both worlds. You allow your team to nominate people who they think have the ability to be effective leaders. I've included an example of a sheet you might use called the Top Three Leaders List. With this method, you take your athletes' recommendations very seriously and get the final word in making the decision. The majority of the time you will simply find that you are endorsing their choice(s) for team captain. This option was used by 16% of the coaches surveyed.

Top Three Leaders List

Fill in the names of up to three teammates who best fit each question. Please be completely honest. You can list yourself if you feel you fit the question.

List the top three people who have the best work ethic on the team:

1._____ 2. _____ 3._____

List the top three people who seem to have the most confidence:

1._____ 2. _____ 3._____

List the top three people who are the most mentally tough:

1._____ 2. _____ 3._____

List the top three people who you trust the most:

1._____ 2. _____ 3._____

List the top three people who care the most about their teammates:

1._____ 2. _____ 3._____

List the top three people who care the most about winning:

1._____ 2. _____ 3._____

List the top three people who help to build your confidence:

1._____ 2. _____ 3._____

List the top three people who unify the team:

1._____ 2. _____ 3._____

List the top three people who are willing to confront and hold teammates accountable:

1._____ 2. _____ 3._____

List the top three people who have the best attitude on the team:

1._____ 2. _____ 3._____

List the top three people whom you respect on the team:

1._____ 2. _____ 3._____

List the top three people who seem to have the best relationship with their teammates:

1._____ 2. _____ 3._____

List the top three people who seem to have the best relationship with the coaches:

1._____ 2. _____ 3._____

4. Seniors automatically named captains.

This option puts the leadership responsibility on the veterans of the group by automatically naming the seniors (or sophomores in junior colleges) as captains. While many times the seniors take this responsibility seriously and rise to the occasion, I can think of several instances where certain seniors were the absolute last people you would want to lead your team. This option also goes against the principle that leadership is a privilege to be earned, not a position to be named. This option was used by 6% of the coaches surveyed.

5. Create a Team Council.

Another option is to have your players choose (or you determine) a Team Council. Team Councils are typically comprised of a representative or two from each class (freshman, sophomore, junior, seniors). In essence, the person becomes a representative or captain for their own class, or can represent their position group (running backs, linebackers, etc. as in a football team). This method usually works well on teams that have larger numbers of people (25 or more). The Team Council meets on a regular basis to monitor the team, give input and feedback to the coaching staff, and make recommendations on any discipline issues. The advantage of this option is that you develop a large number of leaders across your team. The potential drawback of this option is that sometimes leadership by committee can get bogged down. This option was used by 6% of the coaches surveyed.

Former Nebraska football coach Tom Osborne writes in detail about the importance of creating a Team Council in his book *Faith in the Game*. "After the Unity Council was initiated, we won seven consecutive conference or divisional titles and three national championships. I am convinced that exceptional team chemistry was a key factor in this stretch, and that the Unity Council played a significant part in developing this chemistry." If it worked well for Coach Osborne, it could work well for you too.

6. No official captains named.

Finally, some prominent and successful coaches like Tennessee women's basketball coach Pat Summitt and Arizona softball coach Mike Candrea don't designate "official" team captains but allow them to naturally and informally emerge. Coach Candrea tells the team that each of the athletes needs to feel as if she is a leader. The players shouldn't rely on one person to lead them but they all should set the standards for the team. Each person should feel as if she can step forward and lead when necessary. While Coach Candrea does not name specific captains, he does rely heavily on his veterans to set the tone and provide him with input.

This option enables anyone to become a leader and allows leaders to naturally emerge throughout the course of a season. It gives everyone the opportunity to lead rather than deferring to the "official" captains. Most of the time good leaders will eventually step up and assert themselves. However, I have seen some seasons where effective leaders never emerged throughout the entire season. Or, worse yet, the wrong people step forward and try to lead. This option was used by 13% of the coaches surveyed. (Because some coaches never name official captains, I will use the terms "captain" and "team leader" interchangeably throughout the manual.)

How Many Leaders Should You Have?

Another factor to consider is how many leaders you should have. If you coach a large team (25+) and opt to use the Team Council idea, you will have at least four if not up to ten different leaders. As mentioned, this could end up diffusing your team's leadership to the point where it becomes ineffective. With a large team, you may want to have at least two if not three captains. It would be difficult to expect one person to be available for 25 or more people—plus develop solid working relationships with each one of them.

If you have a team of 10-25 members, you may have a couple of people who are legitimate leaders on the team. If so, consider having more than one captain. Basically, the quantity is less important than the quality when it comes to designating team leaders. If you have three athletes who are great leaders and have earned your respect and the trust of their teammates, it would be appropriate to select all three as captains. However, if only one athlete is a legitimate leader, go with only one.

You will often find that one of your captains seems to be a more effective Leader by Example while another might be a more effective Vocal Leader. Hopefully each athlete will be able to utilize their strengths and complement each other for the good of the team.

When Should You Determine Your Team Leaders?

Another factor to consider is when you should determine your team leaders. Here again you have some options. Some coaches determine their team leaders before practices start. This option allows you to establish your team leadership on the front end. Other coaches wait a couple of weeks or even a month into their practices. This allows you the luxury to see how your athletes communicate and compete with each other. It also gives your leaders time to emerge during the early season. Still other coaches like Michigan softball coach Carol Hutchins have their returning athletes determine their leaders for next season immediately following the just completed season. This option provides your team with leaders during the all-important off-season.

What's the Best Way to Determine Your Team Leaders?

So then, what's the best way and time to determine your leaders? Ultimately, after reflecting on the pros and cons of each option, the best way is the one that fits best with your philosophy and the unique makeup of your team. Some coaches even change the way they determine their leaders each season depending on their particular situation. However you do it is up to you. The bottom line is that both you and your athletes need effective, respected, and credible leaders to be successful. Be sure you are doing your part to properly identify, train, empower, and mentor them.

20 Tips for Developing Responsible and Respected Team Leaders

As you read through this manual, you will discover dozens of ideas that you can use to develop your leaders. Here's a highlight list of some of the practical ideas for developing more responsible and respected team leaders.

1. Look for leaders when selecting your team.

Of course you will look for talent when you are recruiting and selecting athletes for your team—but also be on the lookout for leadership ability. Look for athletes who were team captains at other levels, involved with student council, or voted class president. It is much easier to help athletes further develop their leadership skills than to start from scratch.

2. Acknowledge the importance of your leaders.

Let your leaders know how important they are to you and your program's success. Don't be afraid to the let them know how much you will rely on them to set the standards, keep the team focused, and handle conflicts. You may even want to tell them that it is their team. You will be there to help them but ultimately it's the athletes, and in particular the leaders, who determine how far the team will go.

3. Explore your leaders' definition of leadership.

Ask your leaders to describe their philosophy of leadership and what it means to be an effective leader. Their experience of leadership might be quite different from yours. Talk about the leaders whom they respect in their lives and why. Also ask them about leaders they don't respect and why. This will give you tremendous insights into their model of leadership. (See Chapter One for more info.)

4. Discuss what you expect of your leaders.

Sit down with your leaders to discuss exactly what you expect from them. Let them know their responsibilities and how you expect them to conduct themselves. Clarifying your expectations and their roles ahead of time will greatly minimize problems down the road. (See Chapter One for more information.)

5. Discuss the risks and hazards of being a leader.

Talk frankly about the inherent challenges and problems your leaders are likely to face. They will have to deal with conflict, they won't always be liked, and they are always being watched. Be sure they understand that these challenges go with the territory and that they have to be willing to handle them. (See Chapter One for more information.)

6. Provide captains with opportunities to lead.

Look to provide your captains with various opportunities to lead the team. Let them run warm-ups before practice. Let them make any announcements that need to be made for the benefit of the group. Have them call their teammates to inform them when you have changes in your schedule. You can even involve them as leaders in various drills that you will use throughout practice. Or take it a step further and let them plan a practice from time to time. Duke women's basketball coach Gail Goestenkors even assigns her players to scout opponents and provide scouting reports along with the coaching staff. Give them as many opportunities as reasonably possible to help them become better leaders.

7. Give captains input on decisions.

Solicit your captains input on decisions that affect the team. These decisions can range from minor choices like where to eat after the game to major ones like giving their input on how to handle discipline situations. The more responsibility and input you give them, the better leaders they will become.

8. Encourage your leaders to build a relationship with each teammate.

Encourage your leaders to invest the time to build a working relationship with each of their teammates. Just as you need to know each of your players as a coach, so too must your captains be able to relate to each of their teammates. (See Chapter Seven for more information.)

9. Confidentially discuss the psyches of each team member.

Once you have built a sufficient level of trust with your captains, *confidentially* discuss the mindsets of each of their teammates. Which teammates are fragile and which are mentally tough? Which athletes are lazy and which are committed? You and your captains should know what motivates and frustrates each of the players on the team. (See Chapter Seven for more information.)

10. Discuss various approaches to conflict.

Talk with your leaders about potential conflict situations which might arise as well as some potential ways to handle them. This could range from ignoring it to an all out confrontation. Your leaders need to know they have a choice in how they handle conflicts on the team—and the likely consequences of their choices. (See Chapter Ten for more information.)

11. Have frequent discussions, chats, check-ins.

You and your leaders should communicate frequently. In fact, one of the primary purposes and benefits of this 10-week program is that it provides you and your captains with frequent opportunities to interact and discuss important topics. Whether you designate specific meeting times or check-in with each other informally, you will need to continually be on the same page to be effective.

12. Encourage your captains to share their insights with the team.

Your captains will often share their insights and opinions with you in individual meetings. When appropriate, encourage them to share these thoughts with the rest of their teammates. Rather than you doing all the communicating, encourage your captains to tell their teammates things that you both feel they need to hear.

13. Support your captains—be there for them.

Since being a captain is an extremely challenging job, especially for teenagers and young adults, you need to be there for them. They will have internal and external struggles throughout the season. They will be torn between meeting your expectations and their desire to be liked and accepted by their teammates. Understand this and help them work through it. You also will need to watch their backs and back them up when they confront their teammates. They need to know that they have your complete support and trust.

14. Give your captains leadership roles in school and in the community.

Nominate your captains for positions where they will be seen as leaders by others. You can have them to run for Student Council, nominate them for the Student-Athlete Advisory Council, get them involved in a Captain's Council, and encourage them to get involved with community service opportunities.

15. Start early grooming future leaders.

Start early to identify athletes who have the potential to develop into future leaders for your team. Give them some small responsibilities to see how they handle them. Also, encourage them to learn what to do and what not to do from your more experienced and established leaders. You must continually look to develop new leaders to put into your leadership pipeline so that you don't have a leadership void when your current leaders leave the program.

16. Look to develop leaders in key positions.

Certain positions in specific sports virtually demand effective leadership: point guard in basketball, setter in volleyball, quarterback in football, shortstop, pitcher, catcher, centerfielder in baseball and softball, goal keeper and center midfielder in soccer. Pay special attention to develop leaders in these positions. When the talent is relatively equal in these key positions, give the nod to the athlete who is the best leader.

17. Look to give non-starting seniors a leadership role when possible.

Almost every team has at least a couple of seniors/veterans who don't get much playing time. It's easy for these seniors to mentally check out from the team or become negative team leaders. Rather than alienating them, see if they might be worthy of a leadership role. Provided that they deserve it, this leadership role gives them an important responsibility to take pride in and helps them feel like they are a valuable part of your team even though they might not play very much.

18. Appreciate your leaders often.

Because being a team leader can be such a demanding and difficult job, invest the time to let your leaders know how much you appreciate their help. A sincere "thank you" from time to time will do wonders to maintain your captains' morale and motivation.

19. Be careful how you treat your captains in front of the team.

Most of the time you will be more demanding of your captains. However, be careful when you praise them in front of the team. Doing this once in a while is okay but be careful not to do it too often or the rest of the team will come to resent you and the captains. Your other athletes may be jealous and think you are playing favorites.

20. Model effective leadership as a coach.

Last but certainly not least, the best way to develop team leaders is to model effective leadership principles yourself. Your prospective and current team leaders will learn infinitely more about leadership by your actions than what you preach to them. Be sure that you are just as demanding, if not more, of your own leadership skills as you are of your captains. Be sure that you are a Leader by Example and a Vocal Leader yourself.

Are You Up for the Challenge?

In our book for coaches on leadership called *The Seven Secrets of Successful Coaches*, my co-author Greg Dale and I interviewed dozens of top coaches across a variety of sports and levels in an effort to discover their secrets of success. We had the privilege of speaking with Mike Krzyzewski, Pat Summitt, Jerry Yeagley, Mary Wise, Roy Williams, Mike Candrea, and numerous others. Even though they have different personalities and styles of coaching, we discovered that these highly respected and successful coaches have seven qualities in common:

Seven Secrets of Successful Coaches

1 Character-based—credible coaches are people of great character.

2. Competent—credible coaches know the strategies and skills of their sport.

3. Committed—credible coaches have a real passion for coaching.

4. Caring—credible coaches care about their athletes as people.

5. Confidence-builder—credible coaches help athletes feel good about themselves.

6. Communicator—credible coaches communicate and listen well.

7. Consistent—credible coaches have consistent philosophies and moods.

It is these seven qualities which form the foundation of their credibility with their athletes and staff. Because of the leadership skills these coaches demonstrate, athletes want to join their teams, work hard for them, and win for them. Ultimately, we challenge all coaches to be the kind of leader who people want to follow.

However, in this manual, I challenge you to go a step further. If you want to be a great coach, not only must you be a coach who creates followers; you must also be a coach who creates leaders. My hope is that this manual will provide you with a practical program to develop leaders who will make a difference on your team, and more importantly, in the game of life.

"You will go to the highest level only if you begin developing leaders instead of followers."

JOHN C. MAXWELL, AUTHOR OF
THE 21 IRREFUTABLE LAWS OF LEADERSHIP

Welcome to *The Team Captain's Leadership Manual*. Whether you are already a team captain or aspire to be one, this one-of-a-kind manual will provide you with a wealth of practical insights, tips, and strategies to help you become an effective team leader.

As I hope you already realize, being a team leader is both an extreme honor and challenge. In the words of the Peace Corps slogan, "It's the toughest job you'll ever love."

Throughout this manual, you will discover what it takes to be an effective team leader, how to gain both your coaches' respect and your teammates' trust, how to motivate and inspire your fellow athletes, how to handle difficult situations, and how to lead your team to greatness. Along the way, you'll hear about what it takes to be an effective team leader from a variety of respected athletes like Aaron Rodgers, Robert Griffin III, Drew Brees, Trey Burke, Julie Foudy, and coaches such as Mike Krzyzewski, Nick Saban, Tony Dungy, Joe Torre, Pat Summitt, Mike Candrea, Lauren Gregg, Urban Meyer, and Rick Pitino.

The Importance of Effective Team Leaders

How important are good team leaders to a team's success? Just about every coach will tell you that having great team leaders is one of the most important keys to success. Sure, your coach's leadership is important, but most of them will readily admit that they must have at least one leader emerge within the team itself to truly be successful. Here's what some very successful and respected coaches have said about the importance of team leadership:

"Talent is important. But the single most important ingredient after you get the talent is internal leadership. It's not the coaches as much as one single person or people on the team who set higher standards than that team would normally set for itself. I really believe that that's been ultimately important for us."
MIKE KRZYZEWSKI, DUKE MEN'S BASKETBALL COACH

"Talent will get you about seven or eight wins. Discipline will start pushing that to nine. Then when you get leadership that's when the magic starts happening. It's when you start getting rings and some really cool things are happening to your team."
URBAN MEYER, OHIO STATE FOOTBALL COACH

"Teams that have strong leadership have a decided advantage. If you look at the great NBA teams of the past 15 years, one of the common threads is they all had great veteran leaders . . . Each had his own style but they all demanded excellence from the people around them. Not just once in a while, not just when things were going well for them, but all the time."
RICK PITINO, LOUISVILLE MEN'S BASKETBALL COACH

"The key to being successful is to have great leadership on your team. It takes a lot of maturity and a lot of players who are interested in the welfare of the team, who are willing to try and influence and inspire other players on the team to help everybody do what they need to do."
NICK SABAN, ALABAMA FOOTBALL COACH

"Having great leadership is a big key to success. It's really the leaders' team because they are the ones who the rest of the players, especially the freshmen, look up to when setting the standards. Our team will go as far as our leaders are willing to take us."
MIKE CANDREA, ARIZONA SOFTBALL COACH
USA SOFTBALL OLYMPIC COACH

"On every team, there is a core group that sets the tone for everyone else. If the tone is positive, you have half the battle won. If it is negative, you are beaten before you ever walk on the field."
CHUCK NOLL, LEGENDARY PITTSBURGH STEELERS COACH

"Because I understand how important leaders are to the success of the team, I've worked hard at selecting the captains and helping them develop the leadership qualities that I feel are important."
JERRY YEAGLEY, LEGENDARY INDIANA MEN'S SOCCER COACH

As you can see, coaches really value the importance of effective team leaders. The leadership role you play for your team often has more impact on your team's success than what you bring to the team as an athlete. Take a moment to let that last sentence sink in . . . **The leadership role you play for your team often has more impact on your team's success than what you bring to the team as an athlete**. What this means is that the contributions you will make as a captain will be just as important, if not more important, than what you will bring with your physical talent and ability. Believe me, your leadership role is that important!

Effective leadership is about a concept called The Power of One. All it takes is one person who is committed, focused, and on a mission to spark an entire team into believing in themselves, working hard, fighting through adversity, playing with unity, and achieving some very special things. **YOU COULD BE THAT PERSON!**

The Walk-on Freshman Who Led Arizona to a National Championship

Can you believe that a 5'11'" walk-on freshman led Arizona men's basketball to a national championship—without playing a single minute in the championship game? It's true. The 1997 Arizona men's basketball team made an amazing run in winning the NCAA Championship. Along the way, the fourth-seeded Wildcats beat three #1 seeds (Kansas, North Carolina, Kentucky) to stun the nation and win the championship. While Miles Simon was deservedly named the tournament's Most Outstanding Player and was pictured on the cover of *Sports Illustrated*, the team's Most Valuable Player and leader was ironically a seldom-used, 5'11" walk-on freshman guard named Josh Pastner.

All season long, despite experts saying the team was too young, Josh believed the team could win the National Championship. When he told his teammates he thought they could win it all they actually laughed at him—at first. But Josh was compelled to make it happen. Since Josh knew that his playing time would be virtually non-existent, he focused on making sure that his teammates were confident, focused, prepared, and mentally tough. He spent countless hours talking with and rebounding for freshmen guard Mike Bibby to help him perfect his jumper. He put in many late nights breaking down tape with the coaches to pinpoint the weaknesses of their opponents so he could mentally prepare his teammates. Josh was committed to doing whatever it would take to help his teammates play at their best.

While he played only a few minutes during the entire season, mostly at the end of lopsided games, Josh contributed to the team in so many critical ways that the players and coaches were convinced they would not have won the championship without his leadership. Despite not playing a single second in the championship game against Kentucky, walk-on freshman Josh Pastner was instrumental in leading Arizona to a national championship. Because of his tremendous leadership skills, Coach Lute Olson actually awarded Josh a full scholarship for the rest of his playing career—and then hired him as an assistant coach when he graduated. If a walk-on freshman can become a respected team leader, surely you can too.

How Can You Become a Better Leader?

Keep in mind that leadership skills are not something you are born with. There isn't a section on your birth certificate that says check here if the person is a leader. Sure certain personalities make it easier and more natural for some people to be leaders. But the bottom line is that you can learn to be a better leader. You can learn how to motivate yourself and others. You can learn how to build people's confidence by giving them positive feedback. You can learn what to say to refocus your teammates when they are struggling. And you can learn how to gain your teammates' trust and your coaches' respect as a leader.

Becoming a better leader is not a quick and easy thing to do, though. It's not something that you can learn and master in a weekend. If you truly want to be a better leader, you must make the commitment to the process of developing your leadership skills. It takes a lot of honest self-reflection, challenging yourself to expand beyond your comfort zone, learning by trial and error, and understanding what motivates and frustrates people. Becoming a better leader is really an ongoing process. This manual will provide you a workable plan and a solid foundation as you develop your leadership skills for many years to come.

"Contrary to the opinion of many people, leaders are not born. Leaders are made, and they are made by effort and hard work."
COACH VINCE LOMBARDI, GREEN BAY PACKERS

How to Use This Manual

The Team Captain's Leadership Manual is designed to provide you with the necessary insights, strategies, and skills to become an effective team leader. If you make a commitment to reading the sections, reflecting on the questions, filling in the blanks, and practicing the strategies, I promise you will become a better leader.

If you are already a team captain/leader:

If you have already been named a team captain, you can use this manual to prepare yourself to handle the variety of responsibilities and opportunities you have been given. Use the ideas and the activities in the manual to help you proactively motivate your teammates and build better team unity. Also, as you encounter problems along the way—and trust me, you will encounter problems—you can use the manual as a way to help you handle them better and resolve them effectively.

If you aspire to be a team captain/leader:

If you are not yet a team captain but would like to be considered a leader on the team, either now or in the future, use this manual as your roadmap for your leadership development. By exploring these issues ahead of time, you will better position yourself to earn your coaches' respect and your teammates' trust when it comes time to determine future leaders.

If you weren't named captain, but you still want to be a leader:

Even if other teammates were named "official" captains, you can still be an effective leader for your team. Remember, true leadership is a privilege you earn and must vigilantly maintain—not a position you are assigned. Use this manual to help you provide "unofficial" yet important leadership for your team.

"Leadership on any team is critical to success . . . Often leadership is awarded by being elected captain by your teammates or selected by the coaching staff. However, not all leaders are also captains, and just because you are not a captain doesn't mean you cannot lead."
LAUREN GREGG, U.S. SOCCER NATIONAL TEAM ASSISTANT COACH

Team Up with Your Coach if Possible

The absolute best way to use this manual is to work on it with your coach. To be an effective team captain or leader, you and your coach need to be on the same page as much as possible. You need to communicate with each other often throughout the season as well as be open enough to listen to each other's points of view. Most importantly, to be a highly effective coach-captain combination, you have to trust each other completely. Going through the manual together provides both of you with a common understanding and language to handle the responsibilities and challenges of leadership together.

Because your coach's support is so important in helping you become a respected and effective leader, you have probably already noticed that I have included a special introductory section for coaches as well. If you haven't read through it, it reminds them how important you are as a captain to the team's success and their sanity. Thus, it highly encourages them to take advantage of the opportunity to work through the manual with you. Completing and discussing the manual with your coach will provide you both with a lot of things to think about as well as a regular time to get together for discussion. Ideally, leadership is an ongoing adventure that you should share with your coach.

A Chapter a Week Teaches You the Leadership Skills You Seek

The manual is divided into ten chapters, each covering a particular aspect of leadership in depth. I suggest you and your coach each read a chapter a week for a ten week period. After you have read the chapter, answered the questions, and completed the exercises, work with your coach to designate a specific time to sit down and discuss it. Pay particular attention to the questions in the chapters and discuss the responses each of you have given so that you gain a better understanding of each other. At the end of the chapter you will be asked to list three to five key points you gained from the chapter to help you reflect on what you learned. You will also find some practical exercises which will help you practice and extend the concepts. These exercises are designed to introduce you to a variety of perspectives on leadership—plus they allow you to develop relationships with other leaders at your school and in your community. And finally, you will have a blank page for taking notes when you discuss the chapter with your coach and/or fellow captains.

Whatever you do, don't try to read the entire manual in one setting or even over a couple of days. Doing so would only overwhelm and scare you. Leadership is a highly complex topic so take your time as you go through the manual to really think about the concepts and let them sink in to your mind. Just as you cannot speed along the harvest, so too must you be patient in your leadership development.

Once you have completed the entire manual during the early part of your season or off-season, you can then use the Captain's Weekly Monitoring Sheets found in the Summary chapter at the end of the manual as a way to continually monitor yourself and the team throughout the rest of the season. I still encourage you and your coach to communicate on a regular basis. You may want to share part or all of your insights with your coach that you list from completing your Captain's Weekly Monitoring Sheets.

If You Must Go It Alone

If for some reason your coach is unwilling or unable to go through the manual with you, you can still benefit by going through it on your own. (In fact, you will probably have an even greater need for the information in this manual if your coach is not interested in helping you.) If this is the case, I would encourage you to get together with a parent, older sibling, or someone else whom you trust and respect to discuss what you are learning. You might even want to find a couple of captains from other teams at your school and go through the manual with them. Or use the manual in your Student-athlete Advisory Council meetings or Captain's Councils. Leadership is often called a lonely position—so be sure to find some trustworthy people whom you can turn to as you take on the challenge of being a leader. Use these people as sounding boards to clarify your thinking and keep you from saying or doing something you might later regret.

Support and Strength for the Leadership Challenge

As you'll discover throughout this manual, leadership is a challenge. That's the reason why I wrote this manual for you. You'll face many obstacles, adversities, and setbacks. You've got to figure out how to motivate people to be at their best, and refocus them when they are at their worst. You will encounter a lot of gray areas as you go—where it will be confusing and stressful to figure out the best thing to do. There may even be times when you are ready to throw in the towel and give up . . . Don't! Not everything will go perfectly for you as a leader and that's perfectly normal and okay.

The reason I wrote this manual for you is because I know how difficult yet critical your leadership role is. My hope is that the strategies, stories, and quotes in this manual will serve as a source of support and strength for you. All I ask is that you give leadership your best shot. Seek the counsel of others along the way, always keep in mind what is best for the team, and stay true to yourself. In doing so you may not reach your goals, but you will gain the respect of many. And ultimately you will gain self-respect—which you'll soon discover is more important than any awards or championships. I admire your courage and commitment and appreciate the chance to share these ideas with you. Thanks for letting me be a part of your leadership journey!

"The credit belongs to the man who is actually in the arena, whose face is marred by dust and sweat and blood; who errs and comes short again and again, who knows the great enthusiasms, the great devotions, and spends himself in a worthy cause; who at best, knows the triumph of high achievement, and who, at the worst, if he fails, at least fails while daring greatly, so that his place shall never be with those cold and timid souls who know neither victory nor defeat."

THEODORE ROOSEVELT

COMPANION ONLINE LEADERSHIP RESOURCE

For more information,
visit www.TeamCaptainsNetwork.com

CHAPTER ONE

EXPLORING LEADERSHIP

UNDERSTANDING THE REWARDS, RISKS, AND RESPONSIBILITIES OF LEADERSHIP

"Leadership is one of the most observed and least understood phenomena on earth."

JAMES MACGREGOR BURNS

L eadership is a complex topic. Although there are thousands of books written on the topic of leadership for business managers, parents, teachers, preachers, and politicians, amazingly few have specifically been geared for you as an athlete. We'll start our exploration of leadership in this chapter by examining what it means to be a leader as well as the various rewards, risks, and responsibilities of leadership.

Defining Leadership

Before we get into the specific skills that you must develop to be an effective leader, let's first explore what it means to be an effective leader. Take a moment to write down your definition of leadership.

What is leadership?

_____

_____

_____

Here's how some of the world's top leadership scholars and politicians have defined leadership:

_____

"The only definition of a leader is someone who has followers."

PETER DRUCKER

"Leadership is the art of getting someone else to do something you want done because he wants to do it."

DWIGHT EISENHOWER

"Leadership is a function of knowing yourself, having a vision that is well communicated, building trust among colleagues, and taking effective action to realize your own leadership potential."

WARREN BENNIS

"Leadership is influence—nothing more, nothing less."

JOHN C. MAXWELL

There are almost as many definitions available for leadership as there are leaders. That's because there are a lot of important ingredients that go into building effective leaders. There is not one single thing that you can do to become a leader. Leadership is based on your doing dozens of little things every day that earn your coach's respect and your teammates' trust.

Who Do You Respect as Leaders?

Now let's take a look at some of the best leaders you've come in contact with over the years. These might be people like your parents, brothers or sisters, coaches, teachers, team captains, ministers, civic leaders, etc.

List the names or initials of three to five leaders whom you respect the most:

1. _____

2. _____

3. _____

4. _____

5. _____

Characteristics of Effective Leaders

After listing the leaders whom you respect, take a moment to think about what makes them so effective as leaders. What kind of people are they? How do they treat you? How do they communicate with you? How do they handle difficult situations? What motivates them?

List the 8–10 characteristics that describe these effective leaders:

1. _____

2. _____

3. _____

4. _____

5. _____

6. _____

7. _____

8. _____

9. _____

10. _____

By examining the characteristics of leaders whom we respect in our lives, we begin to see some of the major qualities it takes to be an effective leader. By recognizing why we respect them so much, we also learn what it will take for us to be an effective leader. (Similarly, much can be learned by reflecting on poor leaders and their characteristics as well.)

"One of the best ways to pick up leadership qualities is to draw from the leaders in your midst. Ask yourself who strikes you as being a great leader. Observe how they go about their business, try to put your finger on what makes them inspiring leaders."

JOE TORRE, FORMER NEW YORK YANKEES MANAGER

How Do You Perform and Feel with Effective Leaders?

Now take a moment to list what it is like to be led by effective leaders. How do you perform when you work with these leaders and how do you feel about yourself?

1. _____

2. _____

3. _____

4. _____

5. _____

Great Leaders Bring Out Your Best

If you are like most people, you probably feel as if you played your best when being led by respected leaders. You likely felt very confident and capable. You trusted yourself and played aggressively. You weren't afraid of making mistakes and you were willing to take intelligent risks. You demanded your best and worked hard to achieve it. You not only wanted success for yourself, but you also wanted to succeed as a way to honor and appreciate what the person had done for you.

As you think about what the leaders in your life mean to you, you probably have a very deep respect for them as well as a strong emotional bond with these people. They are people who in many cases have had a significant impact on your life. So much so that you might not be the person you are today if it weren't for their guidance, support, challenge, and leadership.

If you haven't already, I encourage you to take time out to write, call, or visit the leaders whom you respect and who have made a big difference in your life. Let them know what a key influence they have had on you and take the opportunity to thank them for it. It's the least you can do for the positive impact they have had on your life. They may also be someone to talk with as you work through this leadership manual.

Inevitably, there is usually a person or two on your list whom you can't talk with directly anymore because they have passed away. This is all the more reason to let those who are still around know how important they are and how grateful you are to them.

Leadership Is Bringing Out the Best in Others

The ultimate goal of leadership is to make those around you better. Leadership is not really about you. Instead, true leadership is about your teammates and what you can do to get them to consistently play to their potential and make smart choices. It is setting them up for success and being as happy for them when they succeed as when you do yourself. Instead of being jealous of their success, celebrate it with them. In actuality, when you help your teammates succeed, everyone succeeds.

"To be a great leader is to make everyone better. That's the greatest gift of all. To elevate the people around you, to get them to maximize their potential, to get them to reach their dreams... Ultimately, leaders are judged by the success of the people they lead."
RICK PITINO, LOUISVILLE MEN'S BASKETBALL COACH

"I think you build on your leadership every year . . . You're constantly trying to get to know the guys better, trying to push guys, trying to figure out what makes guys tick and find ways to motivate everybody."
MATT STAFFORD, DETROIT LIONS

Rewards of Being a Team Leader

1. Satisfaction of Helping Others Succeed

One of the greatest rewards of leadership is the realization that you played a part in helping someone else be successful. Few things are more gratifying than helping someone grow, improve, and succeed.

Dan Gable is considered one of the greatest wrestlers of all time. As a wrestler at Iowa State, Gable won 182 matches over his career with only one loss. He was a two-time NCAA National Champion, a three-time Big Eight Wrestler of the Year, and a Gold Medal winner in the 1972 Olympics without giving up a single point during any of his six matches. After his athletic career was over, he then coached the Iowa wrestling program to 15 national championships over his 21 years as a coach. When asked what his greatest achievement was, Coach Gable said that his accomplishments as a coach far outweighed anything that he achieved as an individual. Take this lesson to heart: leading others to success is much more gratifying than succeeding on your own.

2. Ability to Significantly Impact Your Team's Success

As a team leader, you have the ability to *significantly* impact the ultimate success of your team. You have the power to shape the team's mindset and chemistry in a multitude of ways. Your leadership determines your team's attitude, work ethic, confidence, composure, mental toughness, chemistry, and commitment. With the help of your coach, it is your job to create the kind of team environment that is engineered for success.

3. Position You for Future Leadership Roles

Overall, your experience as a leader can be one of the best and most fulfilling experiences of your life; one which will ideally prepare you to succeed in virtually any kind of future leadership role that you might play in the professional world, as a parent, and/or in your community. (Author's note: Sure, one of my goals in writing this manual was to help you be a better captain for your team. But I'm also banking on the fact that the leadership skills you will develop will go much further than that. Ultimately, my hope is that you not only help your sports team be successful, but that you also use these skills throughout your life to help your family, community, and world be more successful.)

If you're in high school, colleges will look very favorably on the leadership experiences you have on your application. It will certainly be a plus for you during the admissions process because schools love people who have demonstrated leadership skills. For college students, your leadership experience will distinguish you from other candidates in the eyes of prospective employers. Being able to list that you were the captain of your team shows employers you have earned the respect of your coach and peers and gives you a powerful advantage in the competitive job market.

Risks of Being a Team Leader

Obviously, when there are rewards of leadership there are also some risks involved as well. Being a team leader can be one of the most challenging experiences you will ever face. It is only fair that we also explore the potential risks of being a team leader. You must understand the risks up front so that you can decide now whether or not you think you are up for the challenge.

"You've got to deal with egos and attitudes. You've got to deal with behaviors and know when to get a guy involved, to know when to pull a guy to the side, know when to be positive, know when to motivate, and know when to criticize. All these things factor into being a leader."

ANDRE MILLER, DENVER NUGGETS

1. You Will Constantly Be Watched

Leadership is a full-time job. You must be "on" 24 hours a day, seven days a week. You must continually conduct yourself in a manner that earns the respect of your teammates and coaches. This means you can't take a day off at practice. This means you can't act like a fool on the weekends. This means you must get the job done in the classroom. This means you can't cut corners in the weight room. Everything you do is being noticed by someone and has an impact.

"A leader can't make excuses. There has to be quality in everything you do. Off the court, on the court, in the classroom."

MICHAEL JORDAN, CHICAGO BULLS

2. Trust and Respect Are Extremely Fragile

Earning your coaches' respect and your teammates' trust takes a long time. It is a process that could take weeks, months, and even years. However, respect and trust are extremely fragile concepts. One cutting remark, lie, indiscretion, or unethical act could destroy your credibility in an instant. Therefore, you must be very careful to preserve your integrity and your relationships with your coaches and teammates. Once you lose your team's trust and respect, you might never get it back again. And once trust and respect are gone, you cease being a leader.

3. You Won't Always Be Liked

As a leader, you will be put in situations to do and say some things that won't always be popular with all of your teammates. Your job is not to be the most popular person on the team. Your job is to do what is necessary and what is right. That's the only way you'll gain respect. As the saying goes, remember that you can't please all of the people all of the time.

4. Some Teammates Might Be Jealous of You

Some teammates may be jealous of your leadership role on the team. They might feel that they deserved to be captain and are upset because they weren't selected. Others could be jealous of the special relationship you will likely have with your coach. Whatever the case, understand that there may be some teammates who resent you and your leadership role.

5. You Must Deal With Conflict

It will be virtually impossible to avoid dealing with conflict as a leader. Various conflicts will crop up between teammates and coaches over the course of the season and you will need to manage and minimize them. We will talk about several strategies you can use to resolve these constructively, but there is always a risk that someone's feelings could get hurt in the process, possibly yours.

6. You Will Take the Heat When Things Go Wrong

You will take the heat when things go wrong but you might not get the credit when things go well. Leadership is often a thankless, unnoticed, underappreciated job.

7. You Will Be Between a Rock and Hard Place

You may find yourself in some difficult situations between your teammates and your coaches. As a leader, you are expected to be the mediator between each of these groups. Each of them will have slightly different expectations and demands of you. At times you will feel torn in different directions.

8. You Might Be Disappointed

Finally, as a leader, you will be investing a lot of yourself in the success of the team. It feels great when you and your team reach your goals during the season. And conversely, it hurts deeply when you fall short. It's the risk that people take when they pour their heart and soul into any endeavor. You'll discover that taking the leadership risk and possibly falling short is much better than not taking the risk and living the rest of your life with regrets.

Again, look over these risks and understand that they are part of the job description of being a team leader. Whatever concerns you the most should help you become more aware of areas to develop in your leadership skills. You must know that they come with the territory. Decide now whether or not you think you can handle these risks.

Which of these potential risks concerns you the most?

_____

_____

_____

Are you willing to take on a leadership role despite these potential risks?

_____

_____

_____

If you aren't prepared to handle the potential risks that come with the job, let your coach know ahead of time, preferably before captains are determined. There's no shame in admitting that you don't feel you are ready for the numerous responsibilities leadership entails.

Responsibilities of Team Leadership

Being a captain is all about taking responsibility—for yourself and your team. As a team leader, you will have a multitude of responsibilities that you will be required to fill. Your coaches will expect you to fill certain roles while your teammates may want you to fill others. Here are some of the things your coach will likely expect from you:

1. Lead drills, warmups, etc.

At the very minimum, most coaches will expect you to lead the team in warmups and drills during practices. They will expect you to get your teammates organized and keep everyone in line, literally and figuratively.

2. Set the mental and emotional tone for the team.

Your coaches will look to you to set the tone of the team for practices and competition. They will expect you to start practices off right with the right attitude, focus, and work ethic. They also will look to you to refocus the team when practices get sloppy. They will look to you to create a positive momentum going into competition. And change the momentum when it isn't going your team's way. You must be the mental and emotional catalyst for your team.

3. Keep the coaches informed about team issues.

As a team leader, your coaches will expect you to keep them informed about issues that impact the success and psyche of the team. They will want to know such things as: who might be in conflict with whom, how athletes are accepting their roles, if anyone's social life is getting out of control, etc. Of course, your coaches don't need to know every little thing that is going on. You'll have to use your discretion to decide which ones might have an impact on the team. Also, you have to be careful to respect the trust of your teammates as well. You don't want to be viewed as a tattletale.

4. Provide input on team decisions.

Because of your leadership position, your coaches might ask for your input on a variety of decisions that will affect the team. This could include minor decisions like what practice time works best or at which restaurant would the team prefer to eat. Or it could involve more serious issues like how best to discipline a teammate who has broken the team rules. Whatever the case, your coaches will look to you to add your insights to help them make decisions that are in the best interest of the team.

5. Talk with struggling teammates.

Your coaches will expect you to talk with teammates who might be struggling with their performance or role on the team. It is your job to understand them, support them, challenge them, and figure out what you can do to get them back on track. Because you are roughly the same age as your teammates, some of them might be more likely to talk to you about problems that are bothering them rather than your coaches. Good coaches will trust you to give teammates the guidance they might need.

6. Handle conflicts within the team.

Many coaches will want you to get involved with team conflicts when they arise. They believe it is your job to find out exactly what is going on and then find a workable solution to the problem. Many times the problems are small and you can solve them on your own without your coach's help. However, there will be some situations where your coach will be the best (and only) person to properly take care of the problem.

"During the championship years, the most important leaders were Bill Cartwright and Michael Jordan. I relied on them to solve minor problems and give me an accurate reading of what was going on with the team."
PHIL JACKSON, CHICAGO BULLS/LOS ANGELES LAKERS

7. Plan team activities.

Some coaches will expect you to act as the team's social coordinator. It will be up to you to plan and coordinate various events so that your teammates can get to know each other better and bond. They will rely on you to initiate these events as well as make sure that everyone is invited and involved.

8. Be loyal to the coaches and support their decisions.

This expectation will likely be number one on your coaches' list. As a captain, your coaches will put their trust in you. They will probably tell you things that they will not tell your teammates because they respect and trust you. Your coaches will expect you to respect and support their decisions to the team. You might disagree with them behind closed doors, but they will expect you to show a united front to the rest of the team. They also will insist on your loyalty and that you never bad mouth them to your teammates. There must be a sacred trust between you and your coach. Don't do anything that might break this trust. If this is going to be a problem for you, you need to let your coach know now. Although this might be difficult, you owe at least that much to your coach and your team.

Clarifying Your Coach's Expectations

Be sure to sit down and talk with your coach to ask him/her about your responsibilities. Investing the time to clarify exactly what your coach expects from you on the front end will help to prevent a multitude of problems down the road. Ask your coach:

Which roles are the most important for you to play?

1. _____
2. _____
3. _____

Which roles are the least important for you to play?

1. _____
2. _____
3. _____

Are there any other expectations that aren't on the list?

1. _____
2. _____
3. _____

Teammates' Expectations of Leaders

Your teammates will also have certain expectations of you as a captain. Their expectations will include many of the ones already mentioned as well as some of the others listed here.

1. Be the spokesperson for the team.

Your teammates will expect you to occasionally go to your coaches with various concerns/problems they might have. Because coaches are in a position of authority and decide roles and playing time, some athletes are reluctant to speak with them. They might rely on you to help them communicate their thoughts to the coaching staff because they feel uncomfortable doing so.

2. Keep it confidential.

Be careful never to put yourself in a situation where your teammates think you are a spy for the coaches. Some captains try to get in their coach's good graces by reporting every little misdeed their teammates commit. Some coaches may even press you for this information. However, once your teammates perceive you as a tattletale, word will quickly spread and you will lose their trust and respect, probably for the rest of your career.

Your teammates expect you to keep their conversations with you confidential. They want to know that they can trust you and that you won't immediately go running to the coaches every time a teammate has a concern or problem. The quickest way to lose respect as a captain is to tell someone else what a teammate told you in confidence.

Further, respecting confidentiality means keeping team issues within the team. Don't air your team's "dirty laundry" with others in public, especially the media. Sure it would be easy to tell friends from other teams about the problems your team might be having. But stories and rumors spread and get exaggerated quickly within athletic departments and schools. Keep your problems within the team.

Of course, there are a few exceptions to this rule. If a teammate told you that he or she was planning to seriously harm himself/herself or someone else, it would be more than appropriate to involve your coach and/or others. Ultimately, trust your intuition to decide if the matter is something that requires more serious help. If you aren't sure whether or not you should say something, consider talking to a guidance counselor, a counselor at the counseling center, or a trusted friend. You can talk generally about the issue without mentioning specific names.

The bottom line is that many people will place a variety of demands on you—and they will have high expectations for you to meet them. Keep in mind that leadership is all about taking responsibility—for yourself and your team.

Leadership: Position or Privilege?

How do people come into leadership positions? There are a variety of ways that coaches and teams use to determine their team leaders. Some coaches select the leaders on their own, others have the athletes vote, others automatically name the seniors as captains, and some coaches never name "official" team captains but allow leaders to emerge naturally. (Because some coaches do not determine "official" captains, the terms "captain" and "team leader" will be used interchangeably throughout the manual.)

Regardless of how you have come into a position of leadership, what is vitally important to understand is that **leadership is not a position that someone gives you; it is ultimately a privilege that you must earn and maintain**. Some athletes think that being named captain gives them the right to lead. They think that people will automatically listen to them and respect them because they hold the title or position of captain. Being a captain is so much more than just a title you hold. It is a sacred trust you must cultivate, cherish, and preserve. No one is going to respect you because of your title—they will respect you because of how you conduct yourself and the respect you show them.

"As a captain, all you look for is that the players respect you. You lead by working hard, being an honest player and treating people with respect."
DAN CLEARY, DETROIT RED WINGS

"A good leader gets people to follow him because they want to, not because he makes them."
TONY DUNGY, FORMER NFL COACH

"My strategy was to come in and try to lead by example first. Being a rookie, you don't want to come in talking right away. You can rub a lot of guys the wrong way . . . One thing you can't do as a leader is come out and say you're the leader."
ROBERT GRIFFIN III, CLEVELAND BROWNS

How do you earn your coaches' respect and teammates' trust? How do you get your teammates to want to follow you? Unfortunately, it is not as simple as just doing one thing to gain respect. There are a variety of important actions that you must take to earn the privilege to lead. The rest of this manual focuses on the characteristics you will need to consistently demonstrate to become an effective leader.

Two Kinds of Leaders
Coaches and athletes often talk about two kinds of leaders: Leaders by Example and Vocal Leaders. What comes to mind when you think about these two kinds of leaders? Which of the two best describes your leadership style? As you'll discover, both types of leaders are important for every team and each has certain characteristics associated with it.

Leaders by Example
Leaders by Example lead not by what they say but more in how they conduct themselves. These are the athletes who consistently work hard in every drill, play with pride, keep their cool in pressure situations, and do the right thing on and off the field. Leading by Example involves four main characteristics: commitment, confidence, composure, and character. Specific chapters of this

manual will explore each characteristic in greater detail. Because Leaders by Example lead themselves so effectively, their teammates naturally admire, respect, and try to emulate them.

1. Commitment
- self-motivated and self-disciplined
- one of the hardest workers on the team
- cares passionately about the team's success
- competitive

2. Confidence
- believes in self on and off court/field
- wants to perform in pressure situations
- mentally and emotionally resilient following mistakes

3. Composure
- able to keep emotions in check
- controls negative emotions

4. Character
- does the right thing on and off the court/field
- responsible, accountable, reliable
- honest with coaches and teammates/trustworthy
- treats people with respect

Vocal Leaders
Vocal Leaders display the same commitment, confidence, composure, and character of Leaders by Example, but they go a critical step further in that they are willing to step outside of themselves by verbally encouraging, motivating, challenging, and holding their teammates accountable. They have excellent communication and listening skills. They know when and how to encourage teammates as well as when and how to get tough and enforce the rules. Again, specific chapters of this manual will go into greater depth about the skills necessary to be an effective Vocal Leader.

Characteristics of Vocal Leaders

1. Commitment

2. Confidence

3. Composure

4. Character

5. Encourager

   A. Servant—puts needs of team ahead of their own

   - willingly does the grunt work

   - takes the younger athletes "under their wing"

   - listens and supports teammates

   B. Confidence-Builder—builds the confidence of teammates

   - understands each teammate

   - helps teammates feel good about themselves

   - reaches out to struggling teammates and provides support and encouragement

   C. Refocuser—helps teammates stay mentally tough when faced with adversity

   - emotionally intelligent to sense mood of team

   - refocuses teammates when they are down and distracted

   - communicates a sense of optimism and hope

   D. Team Builder—unifies team around a common goal

   - establishes and focuses team on a common goal

   - helps teammates understand, accept, and feel appreciated for their roles

   - brings team together and builds team chemistry

6. Enforcer—courage to confront

- holds self and teammates accountable to high standards/demanding

- constructively confronts undisciplined teammates

- handles conflict in a firm, fair, direct, and consistent manner

The Team Captain's Leadership Model

Leader by Example
1. Commitment
2. Confidence
3. Composure
4. Character

Vocal Leader
1. Commitment
2. Confidence
3. Composure
4. Character
5. Encourager
6. Enforcer

The Team Captain's Leadership Model

Based on these two kinds of leaders, I have developed the Team Captain's Leadership Model to help you better understand the characteristics of being a Leader by Example and a Vocal Leader. Leading by Example is represented by the four squares in the center part of the model. Ultimately you must be able to lead yourself first before you can attempt to step outside yourself and lead others. The four squares contain the four building blocks that you will need to have in place to be an effective Leader by Example. Each of the four areas is critical to your success. Once you get your own house in order, the outer boxes represent the two additional and critical roles of Encourager and Enforcer that you will need to play to be an effective Vocal Leader. Notice how the Encourager part of the model is three times larger than the Enforcer part. As you will soon discover, good Vocal Leadership means that you will spend roughly 75% of your time Encouraging your teammates and 25% of your time Enforcing the rules.

Which Kind of Leader Are You?

As you look at the descriptions of each kind of leader, you will probably see yourself in one more than another. Based on these two kinds of leaders, I've provided you with a quick self-test that you can take called the Team Leadership Self Evaluation. This evaluation will help determine which kind of leader you are currently as well as highlight your strengths and areas for improvement. Keep in mind that both kinds of leaders are important and valuable to have on a team.

TEAM LEADERSHIP SELF EVALUATION

Using a scale from one to five rate yourself on the following 24 questions.

1 = Strongly Disagree, 2 = Disagree, 3 = Undecided, 4 = Agree, 5 = Strongly Agree

	SD	D	U	A	SA

Commitment
	SD	D	U	A	SA
1. I am one of the hardest workers on the team	1	2	3	4	5
2. I care passionately about the team's success	1	2	3	4	5
3. I am a competitive person who wants to win	1	2	3	4	5

Confidence
4. I believe in myself as a person and my ability to lead	1	2	3	4	5
5. I want to perform in pressure situations	1	2	3	4	5
6. I bounce back quickly following mistakes and errors	1	2	3	4	5

Composure
7. I stay calm and composed in pressure situations	1	2	3	4	5
8. I stay focused when faced with distractions, obstacles, and adversity	1	2	3	4	5
9. I keep my anger and frustration under control	1	2	3	4	5

Character
10. I consistently do the right thing on and off the court/field	1	2	3	4	5
11. I am honest and trustworthy	1	2	3	4	5
12. I treat my teammates, coaches, and others with respect	1	2	3	4	5

LEADER BY EXAMPLE TOTAL (add questions 1–12)

Encourager—Servant
13. I reach out to teammates when they need help	1	2	3	4	5
14. I take the time to listen to my teammates	1	2	3	4	5

Encourager—Confidence Builder
15. I regularly encourage my teammates to do their best	1	2	3	4	5
16. I regularly compliment my teammates when they succeed	1	2	3	4	5

Encourager—Refocuser
17. I communicate optimism and hope when the team is struggling	1	2	3	4	5
18. I know what to say to my teammates when they are struggling	1	2	3	4	5

Encourager—Team Builder
19. I have developed an effective relationship with each of my teammates.	1	2	3	4	5
20. I am a team player who seeks to unify the team	1	2	3	4	5

Enforcer
21. I hold my teammates accountable for following team rules/standards	1	2	3	4	5
22. I constructively confront my teammates when necessary	1	2	3	4	5
23. I am willing to address and minimize conflicts between teammates	1	2	3	4	5
24. I am firm, fair, and direct when dealing with conflicts and problems	1	2	3	4	5

VOCAL LEADER TOTAL (add questions 1–24)

Team Leadership Self Evaluation Scoring Directions

The Team Leadership Self Evaluation is divided into two parts. The top 12 questions help you rate yourself as a Leader by Example. Then the first 12 questions are combined with the final 12 questions to help you rate yourself as a Vocal Leader.

Leader By Example Scoring

The Leader by Example Self Evaluation measures the four critical areas you need to be an effective Leader by Example: Commitment, Confidence, Composure, and Character. To compute your Leader by Example score, add your ratings for the first 12 questions.

12–44 = Not a Leader by Example

45–52 = Solid Leader by Example

53–60 = Spectacular Leader by Example

Your total for the Leader by Example section should at least be 45 if not higher. Anything 44 and below you are probably not successfully leading yourself to earn the respect of your coaches and teammates. The closer you are to 60, the better job you believe you are doing of leading yourself and the more respect you likely will gain from others.

You can also explore your section scores to see how you rate your commitment, confidence, composure, and character. Again your section scores should at least be at an 11 or higher to gain respect.

Vocal Leader Scoring

Once you have computed your Leader by Example score using the first 12 questions, you then need to add up your score for questions 13-24. Compute the score for the second half of the evaluation (questions 13—24) and add it to your score for the first half (questions 1-12). The total score for all 24 questions will give you your rating as a Vocal Leader.

24–89 = Not a Vocal Leader

90–104 = Solid Vocal Leader

105–120 = Spectacular Vocal Leader

Your total as a Vocal Leader should at least be 90 if not higher. Anything 89 and below you are probably not doing an adequate job of leading yourself or others. The closer you are to 120, the more you are doing what is necessary to earn your coaches' respect and your teammates' trust to be an effective leader.

Consider Having Your Coaches and Teammates Rate You

Rating yourself is a good way to start evaluating your leadership skills and style. However, if you really want an accurate and relatively objective view of your leadership skills, consider having your coaches and teammates fill out the same evaluation on you. I have included an adapted copy of the Team Leader Evaluation at the end of this chapter that you can give to your coach(es) and teammates if you choose.

Hopefully your relationship with your coach is strong enough that he/she could give you their honest opinion on how they see your leadership strengths and areas for improvement. If you decide to ask your teammates, be sure you have them fill out the evaluation anonymously so they are much more likely to give you their honest feedback—without the fear of hurting your feelings or hampering their relationship with you. It is probably best to have your coach coordinate this process and add up your teammate's ratings to compute an average score for you.

Then, invest the time to compare your self ratings with those of your coaches and teammates. Examine the areas where you seem to agree as well as areas where there are differences. Use the information for how it is intended—to provide you with insights on how other people view you as a leader. Be proud of and continue to build on the areas where others rate you favorably. Look to develop any areas that others might have rated as concerns for you. Be thankful they have provided you with this valuable information to help you become a more effective leader.

Your Game Plan for Becoming a More Effective Leader

Based on the evaluation(s), take a moment to highlight your strengths and your areas for improvement.

What are your strengths as a leader?

_____

_____

What should you continue doing to maintain and build upon these areas as strengths?

_____

_____

What are your areas to improve as a leader?

_____

_____

What are some specific actions you can take to improve these areas?

_____

_____

Of course, the rest of the manual is designed to provide you with dozens of ideas to build on your strengths as well as give you practical strategies to develop the areas which may need improvement. I've included an additional copy of the Team Leader Self Evaluation at the end of the manual so you can notice and celebrate the improvements you have made over the course of the program.

Be Yourself

Although you have created a preliminary game plan to improve your leadership skills based on the evaluation(s), remember that effective leadership ultimately requires you to be yourself. Good leadership development encourages you to honestly explore your strengths and areas for improvement and provides you with a development plan to become your best. Don't feel that you need to change your personality or become a totally different person. Effective leaders come in all forms from those with magnetic charisma to the strong, silent types. Yes, you should stretch yourself to expand beyond your comfort zone and your fears, but at the same time remain true to yourself and who you are. Your teammates and coaches will respect you for being you—not someone else.

"I think there's a lot to be learned from your teammates and older guys around you. And there are many ways to lead. You don't have to change your personality to be a leader."
ANDREW LUCK, INDIANAPOLIS COLTS

"I can say through almost 40 years of NFL experience that leadership comes in a lot of shapes and sizes. I've had players who were very vocal that were great leaders. I've had players who were vocal that weren't great leaders...So it's not about volume or who's the most talkative guy. It's the guy who does his job and puts the best interests of the team and organization in the lead."
BILL BELICHICK, NEW ENGLAND PATRIOTS COACH

CHAPTER ONE SUMMARY

Being a leader means that you will experience a variety of rewards, responsibilities, and risks—be prepared. Understand that there are two kinds of leaders: Leaders by Example and Vocal Leaders. Use the evaluations in this chapter to help you learn the kind of leader you are now as well as ways to build on your strengths and improve your weaknesses. Finally, remember that leadership is a privilege you must earn and maintain.

KEY POINTS FROM CHAPTER ONE

List three to five major points or insights you gained from this chapter:

1. _____

2. _____

3. _____

4. _____

5. _____

PRACTICAL EXERCISES FROM CHAPTER ONE

1. Interview a captain from another team to get their perspective on the responsibilities, risks, and rewards of being a team leader. Ask them:

- What is your definition of effective leadership?

    _____

    _____

- What does your coach expect from you as a leader?

    _____

    _____

- What do your teammates expect from you as a leader?

    _____

    _____

- What are the best things about being a leader?

    _____

    _____

- What are the toughest challenges about being a leader?

    _____

    _____

2. Interview a coach from another team to get their perspective on the responsibilities, risks, and rewards of being a team leader. Ask them:

• What is your definition of effective leadership?

_____

_____

_____

• What qualities and skills do you look for when determining your team captains/leaders?

_____

_____

_____

• What do you expect from your team leaders?

_____

_____

_____

• What are the toughest challenges for your team leaders?

_____

_____

_____

3. Ask at least five of your teammates what they expect from you as a team leader. Summarize their thoughts here:

_____

_____

_____

4. If you haven't already, invest the time to thank the leaders who have made a big impact on your life. Tell them that you aspire to be an effective leader like them and ask them to share some of their observations and lessons on leadership. Summarize their insights here:

_____

_____

_____

TEAM LEADERSHIP EVALUATION

Using a scale from one to five rate the person listed on the following 24 questions.

1 = Strongly Disagree, 2 = Disagree, 3 = Undecided, 4 = Agree, 5 = Strongly Agree

Name	SD	D	U	A	SA

Commitment

1. is one of the hardest workers on the team	1	2	3	4	5
2. cares passionately about the team's success	1	2	3	4	5
3. is a competitive person who wants to win	1	2	3	4	5

Confidence

4. has confidence in him/herself as a person and his/her ability to lead	1	2	3	4	5
5. wants to perform in pressure situations	1	2	3	4	5
6. bounces back quickly following mistakes and errors	1	2	3	4	5

Composure

7. stays calm and composed in pressure situations	1	2	3	4	5
8. stays focused when faced with distractions, obstacles, and adversity	1	2	3	4	5
9. keeps his/her anger and frustration under control	1	2	3	4	5

Character

10. consistently does the right thing on and off the court/field	1	2	3	4	5
11. is honest and trustworthy	1	2	3	4	5
12. treats teammates, coaches, and others with respect	1	2	3	4	5

LEADER BY EXAMPLE TOTAL (add questions 1–12)

Encourager—Servant

13. reaches out to teammates when they need help	1	2	3	4	5
14. takes the time to listen to teammates	1	2	3	4	5

Encourager—Confidence Builder

15. regularly encourages his/her teammates to do their best	1	2	3	4	5
16. regularly compliments his/her teammates when they succeed	1	2	3	4	5

Encourager—Refocuser

17. communicates optimism and hope when the team is struggling	1	2	3	4	5
18. knows what to say to teammates when they are struggling	1	2	3	4	5

Encourager—Team Builder

19. has developed an effective relationship with each teammate	1	2	3	4	5
20. is a team player who seeks to unify the team	1	2	3	4	5

Enforcer

21. holds teammates accountable for following team rules/standards	1	2	3	4	5
22. constructively confronts teammates when necessary	1	2	3	4	5
23. is willing to address and minimize conflicts between teammates	1	2	3	4	5
24. is firm, fair, and direct when dealing with conflicts and problems	1	2	3	4	5

VOCAL LEADER TOTAL (add questions 1–24)

COACH/CAPTAIN MEETING NOTES

_____

_____

_____

_____

_____

_____

_____

_____

_____

_____

_____

_____

_____

_____

_____

_____

_____

_____

_____

_____

_____

_____

_____

_____

_____

_____

_____

_____

_____

Next Meeting Date:
Time:

HOW TO LEAD BY EXAMPLE

"Mastery of others is strength. Mastery of self is true power."
                                                    LAO TZU

L eading by Example means that you can lead yourself. The foundation of all leadership begins with your ability to effectively lead yourself. Why? You must have your own act together before you try to help others do the same. If you are not walking the talk yourself, you have little chance of getting others to believe in you or follow you. You must be able to earn self-respect for the ability to effectively lead yourself before you can earn the respect of others.

For most college and high school leaders (and adults for that matter), getting and keeping your own stuff together is difficult enough with all of the challenges you must face in your life. Leading yourself is not an easy task. It is human nature to want to take the easy road, to worry too much about what your teammates think, and to get frustrated with yourself and others. Leading by Example demands that you hold yourself accountable to work hard when you are tempted to slack off, to stay positive when you have doubts, and to maintain your focus and composure when things aren't going your way. **If you can't lead yourself, you can't lead others**.

The chapters in Section One give you a variety of tools and techniques that will help you better lead yourself. As mentioned before, Leaders by Example excel in four primary areas which allows them to effectively lead themselves.

- Chapter 2 focuses on Commitment. Leaders by Example are highly committed and self-motivated to work hard.

- Chapter 3 focuses on Confidence. Leaders by Example have confidence in themselves and their ability to lead.

- Chapter 4 focuses on Composure. Leaders by Example maintain their composure during stressful situations.

- Chapter 5 focuses on Character. Leaders by Example do the right thing no matter what the circumstances.

| CHAPTER **TWO** |

COMMITMENT

HOW TO GET AND KEEP YOURSELF MOTIVATED

"One person with a passion is equal to 100 with an interest."
ANONYMOUS

Think of some of the world's most admired leaders . . . Martin Luther King Jr., Gandhi, George Washington, Mother Teresa, Nelson Mandela, Eleanor Roosevelt. While they all came from different backgrounds, races, religions, and eras, they all share one important characteristic—an overwhelming sense of commitment to their cause. These people were compelled to put in the time and energy necessary to advance their cause and achieve their missions. Many of them dedicated their lives. Because of their total commitment, they attracted others who wanted to follow them. Their commitment also provided them with incredible reserves of energy and motivation to battle through the tough times they knew would be an inevitable part of the process.

Similarly, to be an effective team leader you must be committed. You must be willing to invest yourself completely—to give your time, energy, and passion to help your team pursue its goals. Your heart must be in it. Being a leader is something you must feel you want to do—not have to do.

Vision of What's Possible

Great leaders know exactly what they want to achieve. They see what is possible for their teams and make it their mission to attain it. This might be winning a conference, state, and/or national championship. Or it might mean turning around a losing program and earning respect. Whatever the case, great leaders establish an inspiring and meaningful goal they are willing to pursue. They determine a mission, or long term goal that they are passionate about achieving.

What specifically is your team's long-term goal for this season?

_____

_____

_____

Is it challenging enough to truly inspire you and your team?

_____

_____

_____

How realistic is your goal given the time frame and people you have?

_____

_____

_____

"People need to see you. They need to see you. If you are the leader they want to see you and know that you are all for them."
ROBERT GRIFFIN III, CLEVELAND BROWNS

After determining an inspiring goal that is both challenging and realistic, you then must decide how badly you want to get there. The more challenging you set your dream, the more commitment you will need to get there.

Make the Commitment

If you want to be a leader, you must fully commit yourself. Your goal has to be of great importance to you; it must be one of the biggest priorities in your life. You must be so inspired by the goal that you fully commit yourself to making it a reality.

Leadership ultimately is an investment. It's an investment of time, energy, and most of all, an investment of yourself to make your dreams, and those of your teammates and coaches, come true. Leadership requires you to put your whole heart into what you are doing. You must care so much about achieving your goal that you are willing to ethically do whatever it takes to make it happen. You must be so passionate about your goal that you are willing to endure all of the obstacles, challenges, and setbacks that will happen along the way. You have got to be willing to invest in your success.

WEEK
2

How important is your goal to you? How badly do you want to reach it?

_____

_____

_____

What are you willing to sacrifice to reach your goal?

_____

_____

_____

"You can't lead others to a place that you don't want to go yourself."
JIM KOUZES AND BARRY POSNER, AUTHORS OF *ENCOURAGING THE HEART*

Compliant, Committed, or Compelled?
The Commitment Continuum™

I developed a tool called the Commitment Continuum™ to help you understand the kind of commitment necessary to earn your teammates' and coach's respect. The Commitment Continuum™ starts with people who are resistant on the far left and runs through those who are compelled on the far right. Each category describes an increasing level of positive commitment as you move from the left to the right. Let's take a look at the characteristics of each level of commitment.

COMMITMENT CONTINUUM™

Resistant

As the name suggests, resistant people resist being led. They have their own stubborn view of how things should be done and are not open to being influenced. They often do not agree with the team's rules and standards and openly oppose them. They complain about coaches, teammates, workouts, conditioning, etc. Resistant people have not bought into the team's common goal but instead pull in the opposite direction.

Reluctant

Reluctants are not yet willing to buy into the common goal. They hesitantly do what is asked of them, only giving half the effort and enthusiasm. Reluctants take a "wait and see" kind of attitude. They are skeptical about committing to the team because they are often concerned their investment is not going to pay off.

Existent

Existents are there in body but not in mind and spirit. They show up but give little more than their mere presence. Existents are apathetic toward the team and the goal—it is of little significance to them. They go through the motions in practice and play with little enthusiasm. It is surprising that they are still a part of the team because they both contribute and gain very little.

Compliant

Compliants will do what they are told by their coaches and team leaders. They are obedient soldiers who do what is expected, but they lack the initiative to go above and beyond the call of duty. They do enough to maintain whatever standard is set by the leader but they aren't willing to do any extra. In this way, leaders can rely on compliants to do what is asked. However, leaders are also a bit frustrated by compliants because the leader always has to supply the direction and motivation.

Committed

Committed people willingly go the extra mile in order to reach their goals. They are self-motivated meaning that they do not need some one else to tell them what to do—or watch over their shoulder to make sure they are doing it. They take the initiative to do what is necessary to get the job done.

Compelled

No matter what obstacles, adversities, or distractions might stand in their way, compelled people are going to find a way. They won't rest until they get the job done. They prepare, train, and compete at the highest level. This means they never go through the motions or skip workouts, they eat well and get the proper rest, and they take advantage of every opportunity to get better. Compelled people not only have high expectations of themselves, but of their teammates, too. They hold themselves AND their teammates to a higher standard.

Obsessed

Obsessed people get so consumed with achieving a specific goal that they lose their sense of perspective. They unmercifully drive themselves and others crazy in their relentless pursuit of their goals. Obsessed people disregard the need for balance in their lives as well as the importance of a recovery phase in their training. They are prone to pursuing the goal at all costs which might include cheating, eating disorders, using performance-enhancing drugs, and other illegal, unhealthy, and unethical means. While highly committed, these people often lack the necessary perspective and people skills to be respected leaders. There is a fine line between being compelled and obsessed—yet there is an important distinction.

WEEK
2

As you examine these different levels of commitment, it is important to consider the following questions:

In which category would you presently rate yourself? Why?

_____

_____

_____

Where do you think your teammates would rate you? Why?

_____

_____

_____

Where do you think your coach would rate you? Why?

_____

_____

_____

Where do you want to be? How will you get there?

_____

_____

_____

Leaders Must Be Committed or Compelled

If you want to have the chance to be an effective leader, you must be in the committed or compelled category. It's nice if you have rated yourself in either of those two categories. However, if you truly want to be a successful leader, the more important questions are where your coaches and teammates rated you. If they haven't rated you at least at the committed level, you will have a hard time gaining their respect.

Ideally, you might have been rated at the compelled category. If this is the case, your teammates and coaches have a tremendous respect for your commitment to the common goal. In my experience, less than 5% of athletes ever truly reach the compelled level. However, the ones who do are special people who often achieve extraordinary success.

Keep in mind you get to choose what level you would like to commit yourself. You can choose how hard you want to work, how serious you want to be about your goals, and what you are willing to do to attain them. Being able to choose your commitment level is the most important choice you have and should not be taken lightly. Recognize your power to choose your commitment.

The scary part of the Commitment Continuum™ is that Resistants are often team leaders too—negative team leaders. Resistants can exert just as much influence on a team as positive team leaders can—sometimes more. We all have seen teams crumble because of negative team leadership. It is the coach's and the captain's job to work together to help prevent and diffuse the development of Resistants. We'll cover several strategies for dealing with Resistants in the Vocal Leadership section.

Work Hard

Hard work is the natural by-product of commitment. When you commit yourself to achieving a specific goal, you realize that you will need to put in a lot of blood, sweat, and tears to turn your dream into a reality. Because you are committed to achieving your goals, you are willing to put in the necessary work. You won't need someone else to tell you what to do or to watch over you because you are self-motivated enough to do the work. You take responsibility for your training, diet, rest, and everything else that might impact your performance. Instead of seeing these commitments such as conditioning, cutting down on junk food, and having a sensible social life as short-term sacrifices, you should view them as long-term investments in your dream.

Hopefully your teammates will admire your commitment and your example will motivate them to follow your lead. Some of your teammates will raise their level of commitment; however, not all of them may react this way. Some of your less committed teammates, those in the compliant level and below, might even attempt to sabotage your commitment efforts. They might make fun of you for your high commitment. Or they might attempt to embarrass you into backing off by saying that you are making the rest of them look bad. Some of your teammates, for whatever reason, will not always share your commitment and work ethic. As a leader you are facing a formidable foe—human nature that is filled with laziness, jealousy, and mediocrity. Stay true to yourself.

"First in, last out. That sums up the leadership code of the FDNY. Like most other leadership principles, it's a simple concept, but one that's difficult to live up to. To be the first in and last out will earn the trust of all around you."
JOHN SALKA, FDNY FIRE CHIEF

"The second I let down, particularly if I'm perceived as the leader of my team or my company, I give others an opening to let down as well. Why not? If the person out front takes a day off or doesn't play hard, why should anyone else?"
MICHAEL JORDAN, CHICAGO BULLS

WEEK 2

Play With Passion and Enthusiasm

Great leaders also display tremendous passion and enthusiasm. As a Leader by Example, it will be your job to bring your energy to the team. Let your love for your sport shine through and be contagious with your teammates. Come to practice with a smile on your face and ready to work hard. Enjoy the challenges that practices offer and make them fun for yourself and your teammates. Yes, practice is work but you can make it fun by challenging yourself and your teammates to have fun with it too.

When you sense the energy level is down on your team, it will be up to you to get it cranked back up again. Many sports are greatly impacted by momentum. It is up to you to bring your passion and enthusiasm to your team to get the momentum back on your side. Be sure that your enthusiasm is contagious. We'll talk more about how you can generate positive momentum in the Vocal Leadership section.

Competitiveness—Instill Your Will

Dehydrated and dizzy because of food poisoning and a stomach virus, Michael Jordan still carried the Chicago Bulls with his competitiveness to an important Game Five win in the Delta Center against the Utah Jazz in the 1997 NBA Finals. Even though he could barely stand, Jordan put the Bulls on his back playing 44 minutes and scoring 38 points, including the game-winning three-pointer in the final seconds. Said Bulls teammate Scottie Pippen, "I've never seen Michael as sick as he was, to the point where I didn't think he was going to be able to put his uniform on. The effort he came out and showed us was incredible. He's not only the greatest player ever, but he's the greatest leader ever."

You will need to have a strong competitive will as a leader. While you can keep the game in perspective, winning is one of your primary goals. Why would you invest so much of yourself and put in all the work if winning wasn't important to you? As former Detroit Pistons star Isiah Thomas said, "Basketball is less a battle of skills and more a battle of wills." The same holds true for any sport.

Losing is basically not an option for most leaders. It's almost as if you can will your team on to victory. Whether you make a big play at a crucial moment to spark your team, or keep your teammates focused under pressure and inspire them to come through in the clutch, you must have a "refuse to lose" mentality.

"You can take the best team and the worst team and line them up and you would find very little physical difference. You would find an emotional difference. The winning team has a dedication. It will have a core group of veteran players who set the standards. They will not accept defeat."
MERLIN OLSEN, FORMER NFL PLAYER

Leaders take the attitude of "Lead, follow, or get out of my way." They model the attitude of "Step up or step aside" and "Go hard or go home." It's your job to instill your will in your teammates. You must make every effort to get your teammates on board, but you also must be willing to go it alone if necessary from time to time, too.

It is this strong competitive will that transforms leaders by example into Vocal Leaders. Leaders by Example try to lead by how they conduct themselves. However, there often comes a point where leading by example is not enough. A person's strong competitive drive often is the key variable that forces them to speak out and lead their teammates. We'll talk more about this in Section Two.

"On most clubs, the leaders are the veteran guys. The young guys are too busy worrying about their stats, establishing their careers, playing for that next big contract. They have priorities other than winning. You want your leader to be someone who's all about winning."
JEFF BAGWELL, HOUSTON ASTROS

"I win, Coach. That's what I do."
TREY BURKE, WASHINGTON WIZARDS

Chapter Two Summary

Leaders must be committed. Develop a challenging yet realistic vision of where you want to take your team. Get your teammates excited about what is possible, then make a full commitment to pursue it with all your heart and soul. As Kenny Rogers once sang, "When you put your heart in it; it can take you anywhere." Play with passion and enthusiasm as you look to instill your competitive will in your teammates.

KEY POINTS FROM CHAPTER TWO

List three to five major points or insights you gained from this chapter:

1. _____
2. _____
3. _____
4. _____
5. _____

PRACTICAL EXERCISES FOR CHAPTER TWO

1. Find and interview someone who you think is compelled. Ask them:

- What motivates/drives you?

_____

_____

- How important is success for you?

_____

_____

- How do you handle it when others don't seem as committed as you are?

_____

_____

2. Rate each of your teammates on the Commitment Continuum™ Put their initials under the level of commitment which best describes them.

COMMITMENT CONTINUUM™

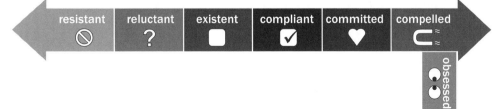

Why do you think each person is where you put them?

_____

_____

_____

What can you do as a leader to help your teammates become more committed?

_____

_____

_____

3. Ask your coach to honestly rate you on the Commitment Continuum™. Be sure that your coach tells you the reasons for the rating.

Do you agree with your coach's rating? Why or why not?

_____

_____

_____

Do you ever find yourself in the obsessed area?

_____

_____

_____

If yes, when and why?

_____

_____

_____

4. Ask your teammates to anonymously rate you on the Commitment Continuum™. (Have your coach coordinate this for you. You may even want to have everyone anonymously rate all of their teammates and coaches, too. If you do, your coach should give everyone their results privately.)

To learn more about building your and your teammates' commitment, check out our six-week *Commitment Continuum System* at www.janssensportsleadership. com.

COACH/CAPTAIN MEETING NOTES

Next Meeting Date:
Time:

WEEK
3

CONFIDENCE

HOW TO BELIEVE IN YOURSELF AND YOUR ABILITY TO LEAD

"One person with confidence is a majority."
ANONYMOUS

In addition to being committed, good leaders have confidence. Having confidence means that you believe in yourself and your ability to lead. This chapter focuses on what it takes for you to have confidence in yourself, both in your sport and in your personal life.

Confidence Is Fragile: Handle with Care

The toughest thing about confidence is that it is such a fragile construct for many people. Former Tennessee coach Pat Summitt recruited and signed many of the nation's best women's basketball players. However, Coach Summitt noticed that even the elite players sometimes struggled with their confidence. "I've realized kids come in here less confident and more fragile." Even former San Francisco quarterback Joe Montana, who led the 49ers to four Super Bowl championships, admits, "Confidence is a fragile thing."

Sports are filled with many ups and downs that can impact your confidence. There is a great deal of natural failure built into virtually every sport. Consider this: the greatest football quarterbacks throw incomplete passes 40% of the time. The top basketball players miss 50% of the shots they take. All-American baseball and softball players don't get a hit 70% of the time. And great hockey and soccer players find the back of the net on only 10% of their shots on goal. Thus you can tell that unsuccessful attempts are very much a real part of every sport. Even the best athletes struggle with their games from time to time and need to repair, rebuild, and restore their confidence.

Some captains have a tendency to stop leading when they aren't playing well. Their lack of confidence causes them to retreat into their shells, stop communicating, and actually become a distraction to their teammates. Don't let this happen to you. Use the strategies in this chapter to maintain or regain your confidence whether you have your "A" game or your "B" game.

Solid Sense of Self

Ultimately your confidence must come from within. You must believe in yourself and who you are as a person. This is the only way to get others to believe in you. You have to be comfortable with yourself and like the person you see staring back when you look in the mirror. Certainly I'm not advocating that you be narcissistic, arrogant, or selfish. But you must be comfortable with yourself and accept yourself for who you are.

You might be surprised at how many athletes seem confident in themselves in their sport, but have little or no confidence in themselves as a person. On the field they seem to have it all together, but off the field their life is a complete mess. These athletes often have a hard time transferring their sport confidence into personal confidence.

Athletes who lack personal confidence do not make good leaders. If you worry too much about what others may think of you, then you don't have the necessary confidence to be a good leader. Yes, it is important to care about how others view you. But at the same time you cannot let it dictate your every feeling and action. There will be many times when you must stand up for what is right, go it alone, and follow your convictions. If you worry too much about the opinions of others, then you don't have the courage to be an effective leader. Athletes who focus more on popularity than principles do not make good leaders. They lack the self-assurance and courage that effective leadership demands.

Maturity certainly helps with this process. However, many adults still have not figured out who they are and what they are all about. Thus, it is even a greater challenge to accomplish this at the college and high school levels. Ironically, getting a degree is not the biggest accomplishment for most college students; it is figuring out who they are as a person and what they stand for by the time they don their cap and gown.

How comfortable are you with yourself and who you are as a person?

_____

_____

_____

How much importance do you put on what others think of you?

_____

_____

_____

What do you stand for? What are you all about?

_____

_____

_____

Can you do/say what is right even though it might go against the crowd?

_____

_____

_____

Want to Perform Under Pressure

Confidence is also critical in your sport. As a confident leader, you should want to perform when the game is on the line. Of course, this does not mean that you will make every play or even get the chance to. But your teammates will know that you have the confidence in yourself to go for it. If you shy away from pressure situations, you will quickly lose your teammates' respect. Confident athletes play to win instead of playing not to lose. They aggressively look to make plays. They take intelligent risks without letting the fear of failure overwhelm them.

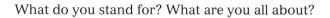

"I want to be the guy this team leans on in crucial situations.
You always hear people saying, 'I'd want to be in a foxhole with that guy,'
that's what it's all about."

BRETT FAVRE, FORMER NFL QUARTERBACK

Four Sources of Confidence

There are four main sources of confidence that athletes use to create, build, and maintain their confidence. Take a moment to look over these four sources of confidence. Then fill in the Strengthening Your Confidence Worksheet with your four sources of confidence.

1. Preparation

One of the biggest and best sources to build your confidence is to remind yourself of the quantity and quality of hard work you've done. Hard work and great preparation are the foundation of confidence. If you have put in the work to better yourself and your game, you deserve the right to be confident. You have paid the price of success. When you know that you have worked just as hard if not harder than the person you are competing against, you have the right to be confident that you can compete with them and beat them. Confidence then is something you earn by all of the quality training you put in. It includes all of your practicing, weight lifting, conditioning, agilities, mental training, nutrition, rest, etc. Take a moment to reflect on and list all of the quality preparation you have done thus far. If you notice some gaps in your preparation, be sure to add these areas in to your practice plans for the next few weeks.

2. Strengths

Another great way to build your confidence is to take an inventory of all the strengths you possess as an athlete. What do you do well? What do you have going for you physically? (speed, quickness, strength, flexibility, endurance, etc.) What aspects of your game are your best weapons? (your curve ball, serve, ball handling, shooting, etc.) What are your mental strengths? (competitive, hard worker, great attitude, persistent, etc.)

Again, I'm not advocating that you be arrogant or cocky. But you do need to know what your strengths are and be proud of them. The strengths are the weapons you do battle with. You must know what you are good at so you can unleash these strengths on your opponents.

In some cases, I have had extremely talented Division I athletes lack confidence so much they felt they didn't have any strengths to list. More often than not, it tended to be female athletes rather than male athletes. I think this is because our society teaches men to project confidence and sureness—even if they don't actually feel this way deep down inside. Unfortunately our society also tends to tell women that they don't measure up if they don't have a cover girl face or the body of a supermodel. Thus, it seems that women tend to struggle with their confidence more so than men.

If you struggle with your confidence because you are a perfectionist, you need to give yourself a break. Stop being so critical of yourself. If you are struggling to write down your strengths, ask someone you trust to help you. Your coaches and teammates will see a lot of strengths that you just aren't giving yourself enough credit for right now. Take their comments to heart and force yourself to be proud of these areas—instead of trying to deny them or feeling embarrassed about them.

3. Past Successes

Reflecting on your past successes is another excellent way to bolster your confidence. Basketball great Michael Jordan used this technique a lot in building his confidence. Whenever Jordan was in a pressure-packed situation, he said he often reminded himself of a shot he hit when he was a freshmen at the University of North Carolina. Jordan's shot helped the Tar Heels win the national championship way back in 1982. Jordan said that he figured if he could hit a big shot in that situation, it would be just as easy to do it again. Similarly, take a look at the key plays you have made over your career. If you could come through in those situations, you have already proven to yourself and others that you have what it takes to be successful. The ability is there physically; you just need to remind yourself of it mentally so that it will surface again when you need it.

WEEK
3

Sometimes, even losses and unsuccessful attempts can be used as a source to build confidence. For example, let's say you played a very close game with a very highly ranked opponent only to lose it on a fluke play or questionable call at the end. Even though it goes in the standings as a loss, you can still use this experience as a way to build your confidence. You proved you could play with the best and had the opportunity to beat them. Use this knowledge and confidence the next time you face them or another higher ranked opponent.

4. Praise

Finally, you can use the words and actions of others to help build your confidence. Think of a time when someone you really respected paid you a compliment. How did it make you feel? Did their belief in you help you believe more in yourself? Hopefully you can look back on your career and remember the complimentary words of coaches, teachers, parents, friends, and others you respect who have acknowledged your ability. Use these compliments to remind yourself that you do have what it takes to be successful.

STRENGTHENING YOUR CONFIDENCE WORKSHEET

What kind of training and preparation have you put in?

1. _____   6. _____
2. _____   7. _____
3. _____   8. _____
4. _____   9. _____
5. _____   10. _____

What are your strengths as an athlete and leader?

1. _____   6. _____
2. _____   7. _____
3. _____   8. _____
4. _____   9. _____
5. _____   10. _____

What past successes have you achieved?

1. _____   6. _____
2. _____   7. _____
3. _____   8. _____
4. _____   9. _____
5. _____   10. _____

Who are some other people who believe in you and support you? List the people and any compliments you can remember them saying . . .

1. _____   6. _____
2. _____   7. _____
3. _____   8. _____
4. _____   9. _____
5. _____   10. _____

Which source do you tend to use the most when looking to build your confidence?

_____

_____

_____

_____

Rely Primarily on Yourself for Confidence

While all four sources can be used to build your confidence, I want to caution you not to put too much stock in other people's praise. It can help you jump start your confidence from time to time. But don't use it as your primary or sole source of confidence. Why? Two reasons. First, confidence must come from within. You don't want to rely on others' opinions of you to determine your level of confidence. Second, you might be in an environment where praise is not given very often. If you need other people to give you confidence and the person who is leading you is not giving out any, your confidence will starve to death. Take most of your confidence from your preparation, strengths, and past successes.

Resilient Reaction To Failure—Optimism

A final way to demonstrate your confidence is how you react to failure. How do you respond when you make mistakes: Do you give up, pout, and make excuses? Or do you learn lessons from them, refocus on the next play, and correct your mistakes? Confident athletes obviously don't like making mistakes, but they quickly recover from them and refocus on the next play with optimism. They project an attitude of "Don't worry about it—I've got the next one."

What do you need to do to bounce back from failure and maintain an optimistic outlook? Martin Seligman has done some excellent work on optimism in a book called *Learned Optimism*. He says the primary key to overcoming adversity is how you choose to view or explain it. Successful people choose to view setbacks as temporary, localized, and changeable. Let's briefly explore each of these to help you become more resilient.

- **Temporary**— "This too shall pass," nicely summarizes this principle. What this means is that no matter how bleak things seem at the moment, sooner or later they will improve. In this way, successful people view adversity as something that occurs during a limited time period. By staying patient and persistent, remember that things will eventually go your way.

- **Localized**—Chicken Little's famous panic-stricken phrase, "The sky is falling, the sky is falling," is the exact opposite of this concept. Like Chicken Little, some people have the tendency to exaggerate problems and extend them into all areas of their lives. They tend to make mountains out of mole hills by panicking over minor problems. Confident people keep their problems limited to certain aspects of their life. This means if you are struggling with your history class, it doesn't automatically mean that you will do poorly on your English paper, too. Keep the adversity you are experiencing in perspective and limited in scope.

- **Changeable**—The statement, "I woke up on the wrong side of the bed today," characterizes those who think that fate controls their lives. Some people believe that they are helpless when it comes to adversity. They feel powerless and that there is nothing they can do to change the situation. Confident people remain optimistic because they know that an adjustment in their approach or mental attitude is often enough to make a difference. They keep trying because they believe they have the ability to influence and sometimes control their own destiny.

So the next time you are faced with a setback, be sure you choose to view it as something that is temporary, localized, and changeable and you will model a powerful sense of optimism for your teammates.

CHAPTER THREE SUMMARY

If you are are going to be a leader, you must be confident in yourself as a player and as a person. Earn your confidence by putting in quality preparation and remind yourself of your strengths, past successes, and the praise you have received. Believe in yourself and your ability to bounce back from mistakes and losses.

KEY POINTS FROM CHAPTER THREE

List three to five major points or insights you gained from this chapter:

1. _____

2. _____

3. _____

4. _____

5. _____

PRACTICAL EXERCISES FOR CHAPTER THREE

1. Make a Success Script for yourself.

   Use the ideas you wrote down on the Strengthening Your Confidence Worksheet. Find some music you like which gets you in a great, positive, upbeat mood. With the music in the background, record yourself saying each of the ideas on your Confidence sheet with conviction. Repeat each phrase three times so that it will sink in. After making the recording, listen to it at least once a day for the next three weeks. You can use it to get ready for practice and to motivate yourself before competition. You'll be amazed at how much your confidence will soar!

2. Interview someone who seems to have a lot of confidence. Ask them:

• From where do you get your confidence?

_____

_____

_____

• How important is confidence to your success?

_____

_____

_____

• Are there times when you lack confidence? When?

_____

_____

_____

• What do you do to build your confidence when you have doubts and fears?

_____

_____

_____

3. Reflect on one of your all-time greatest competitions.

• Where was your confidence going into the competition?

_____

_____

_____

• From what source(s) did you draw your confidence?

_____

_____

_____

- Did your confidence waver at all during the competition?

_____

_____

_____

- What did you think about to maintain or regain your confidence?

_____

_____

_____

COMPANION ONLINE LEADERSHIP RESOURCE

For more information,
visit www.TeamCaptainsNetwork.com

<u>COACH/CAPTAIN MEETING NOTES</u>

_____

_____

_____

_____

_____

_____

_____

_____

_____

_____

_____

_____

_____

_____

_____

_____

_____

_____

_____

_____

_____

_____

_____

_____

_____

_____

_____

_____

_____

_____

Next Meeting Date:
Time:

CHAPTER FOUR

COMPOSURE

HOW TO KEEP YOUR COOL UNDER PRESSURE

"It's the way he carries himself, the way he's always ready, always alert, always into it. When things were going against us he was pulling everybody together. That's the leadership I'm looking for."
TOM THIBODEAU, MINNESOTA TIMBERWOLVES COACH ON DERRICK ROSE

Along with confidence comes composure. Great leaders are able to keep themselves under control during the heat of battle. They effectively manage their emotions and keep themselves on an even keel when everyone and everything else around them might be going crazy. Why is it so important to manage your emotions? Because your teammates will be watching you to see how you handle the situation. Whatever response you show, they will be likely to reflect the same response.

Are you . . .

- panicked or poised?
- disappointed or determined?
- overwhelmed or optimistic?
- frustrated or focused?
- giving up or going strong?
- exasperated or energized?
- scared or self-confident?

51

How you choose to respond to adversity has a big impact on how your team-mates will choose to respond to it, too. Your mindset should be—the tougher it gets, the tougher I get.

---

*"When things aren't going well, it's not what a leader says,
it's how a leader looks that matters."*

MIKE KRZYZEWSKI, DUKE MEN'S BASKETBALL

Traffic Light Analogy

How do you manage your emotions? One of the first steps is better awareness. I like to use a traffic light analogy originated by my good friend and mentor Ken Ravizza in his book *Heads Up Baseball* to help athletes become more aware of their mindset. When you are composed, confident, and in control, we call this a green light. A yellow light is when you become distracted, frustrated, and confused. And finally, for those times when you lose control, are totally flustered, and want to either explode or give up, you've hit a red light. This traffic light analogy will help you become more aware of your mindset as well as provide you with a practical way to better manage your emotions.

- **Green Light:** composed, optimistic, confident, focused, determined, communicating, encouraging, strong body posture, aggressive, poised

- **Yellow Light:** frustrated, questioning, doubts, negative, blaming/making excuses, distant, tentative, distracted, confusion, rattled

- **Red Light:** angry, pessimistic, overwhelmed, out of control, apathetic, hopeless, poor body posture, unapproachable, scared, emotional

Like every athlete, there are times when you experience all three of these mindsets. Odds are you experience at least two if not all three of these traffic light mindsets throughout the course of every practice and competition. It's easy to be in a green when you are playing well. You can fall into a yellow when you are struggling or not getting the calls you feel you deserve. And you can get into a red if you really start fighting yourself and letting things get to you.

Green Means Go

This analogy will help you become more aware of your emotions and how they influence your performance. Obviously a green light gives you the best chance of being successful because your mind is where it needs to be to perform at your best. When you are in a yellow, you start battling yourself because your mind becomes cluttered and confused. In the red, you end up beating yourself because you have lost the mental battle within.

Ultimately you are trying to get yourself into the green and successfully deal with the yellows and reds that will occur. Further, you can use this analogy to gauge the mindset and emotions of your teammates (and coaches). As we will see later, being a Vocal Leader is about your ability to get your teammates into a green and to refocus them when they get into yellows and reds.

Your Lights Are Contagious

Each of these three mindsets not only impacts your performance and satisfaction but your teammates' mindsets as well. When your teammates see you in a green light as a leader, they are much more likely to be in a green light themselves. However, if they see you in a yellow or a red, the majority of them will soon be there, too. **When you Lead by Example, you must realize how contagious your light colors are for your teammates.** The best way to get them in a green is to be in a green yourself.

As a leader you should look to spend as much time as possible in the green light. Shoot for at least 70% of your time in the green, preferably more. You will get to the yellow light from time to time. Shoot for around 20% to at most 33% of the time in the yellow. Try to limit the number of times you get to the yellow as well as how long you stay in the yellow light. For example, you might hope to hit the yellow light only two to three times out of every practice or competition rather than nine to 10 times. Further, when you get to the yellow, the goal is to turn it around as quickly as possible. Transform your mindset in a matter of minutes rather than letting it drag on for hours or even days.

WEEK 4

How to Get Into a Green Light

What do you do before a practice and competition to get yourself mentally ready to perform? Athletes like to do a variety of things before competing in an effort to get themselves into a green light. Here are some of the typical approaches athletes use to get themselves ready to play.

1. Go over the game plan and/or scouting reports.

You might be the kind of player who likes to run through the game plan in your mind before you compete. Go through the scouting report on your opponent and focus on three to five keys that will allow you to be successful.

2. Visualize how you want to play.

You can visualize yourself going through some key moments in your upcoming competition. See yourself aggressively playing the way you want to—executing your game and taking it to your opponent.

3. Quiet reflection/prayer.

You may prefer to sit quietly by yourself as you clear your mind and gather your thoughts on the upcoming competition. If your religious beliefs are a source of strength for you, you will likely spend time in prayer.

4. Listen to music.

You might want to listen to music as you prepare yourself to compete. Music is obviously a highly individualized choice so be sure to bring your headphones.

If you find that you seem to perform better when you are really pumped up and energized, find some music that helps you feel that way. However, if you seem to play better when you are more relaxed and calm, find some more relaxing music. Music is a great way to help you set the mood you want to have going into competition.

5. Chat with teammates.
You might be the kind of athlete who likes to stay loose simply by chatting casually with teammates. You like to relax by joking around with teammates before you play to keep your mind from thinking too much. You know if you went off by yourself in a corner and thought about the competition too much you would probably drive yourself crazy.

6. Watch highlight videos.
A great way to get you confident and energized going into a game is to watch a highlight film of some individual and/or team highlights from past competitions complete with music.

7. Take a nap or a shower before hand.
You might want to be well rested before you play so you look to take a short afternoon nap. Others like to shower before a competition to help them feel refreshed.

8. Team chant.
Many teams like to create and use a special team chant as they prepare themselves to compete.

Ultimately, you want to find something that works well for you. You need to develop a consistent pre-competition routine whether you are playing at home or on the road. If you want to perform consistently, you must prepare consistently.

As a leader, keep in mind that each person prepares a little differently. Thus, remember that what works to get you motivated, confident, focused, and ready to perform might actually be the opposite of one of your teammates. Encourage them to mentally prepare in their own way and give your teammates the flexibility to do whatever works the best for them.

How to Handle Yellows and Turn Them Into Greens
While getting yourself into a green light consistently is important as a leader, the bigger and more crucial challenge is how you choose to deal with yellow and red light situations. It's easy to stay focused and confident when your team is winning, when you are getting the calls, and when you are playing well. The real challenge is how you respond when the "stuff" is hitting the fan—that's when your leadership ability really gets tested. As I indicated earlier, as a Leader by Example, all eyes will be on you to see how you handle the situation.

The key is really the yellow zone. Why? Because as humans it is impossible to stay in the green all of the time. As the sage philosopher Kermit the Frog from Sesame Street once sang, "It's not easy being green." Kermit understood that it is not always easy staying in a green light with all of the adversities, obstacles, and challenges of sport. Thus, the key is going to be your ability to recognize when you are in a yellow. Take a moment to reflect on the past times you were in the yellow.

Describe how you think and feel when you are in a yellow light:

_____

_____

What past events or circumstances might have led you to a yellow light?

_____

_____

Notice I didn't say that these events caused the yellow light—because they didn't. Ultimately it was your interpretation of these events that caused you to go into a yellow light. Thus, you must remember that you control what color light you are in. It's not the situation that causes you to get into a yellow or red light. It's your interpretation of the situation that causes the yellow or red. Change your interpretation and you change your light.

Recognizing and Refocusing in Yellows

Getting yourself out of yellows and reds depends on your ability to refocus effectively. Once you recognize that you are in a yellow, your task is to get yourself back under control. You can do this by refocusing your thinking on thoughts that will bring you back to the green light. If you don't recognize when you are in a yellow and/or you have not developed the ability to refocus yourself effectively, you are likely headed for the red zone. When you drop all the way down into the red, you have really lost control of your mental game. As you might imagine, once you allow yourself to get into a red light, it is a lot tougher to regain control. Thus, it is critical that you catch yourself early in a yellow because it is much easier to refocus when you are in a yellow than when you are in a red.

As a way to help you recognize your mental traffic lights, I suggest you put a green dot somewhere on your uniform, equipment, or even yourself. You can get small round green labeling stickers at any office supply store to stick on your equipment. Or you can take a green marker and put a dot on your shoes or your hands. Whatever the case, put it someplace where you will see it often. This green dot is designed to remind you to monitor your traffic lights as you practice and compete. If you find that you are drifting out of the green light zone, use any number of the upcoming strategies.

Refocusing Strategies

As the originator of the traffic light analogy, fellow sport psych consultant Ken Ravizza also has a simple yet profound observation on peak performance. Ken says, "Peak performance isn't so much about your ability to focus. It's more about your ability to refocus." Think about it . . . The real key to maintaining your composure depends on your ability to quickly and successfully refocus yourself back on the task at hand. Rather than getting caught up in the distractions and frustrations, you must develop some workable strategies to get your mind back on track. Here are a variety of tips and techniques you can use to bring yourself out of a yellow and back to a green.

1. Slow the Pace to Allow Yourself Time to Regroup and Refocus

Start your refocusing efforts by deliberately slowing down the pace at which you play. Tie your shoes, adjust your equipment, tuck in your uniform, get a drink, etc. Do something that will allow yourself some time to get yourself together and break the negative momentum. During this break you can use any of the following mental strategies to refocus yourself.

2. Control the Controllables

When you are in a yellow or a red, things may seem like they are spinning out of control. One of the best ways to regain control of the situation is to regain control of yourself and your thinking. To do this it is important to recognize what you can and cannot control in the situation. Knowing the difference between what you can control (controllables) and what you can't control (uncontrollables) is a key mental skill as a leader. Let's take a look at the uncontrollables first.

Uncontrollables

Uncontrollables are all of the people, factors, and variables you wish you could control as an athlete, but unfortunately, you have little or no control over them. See if you can list at least eight factors that are outside of your control:

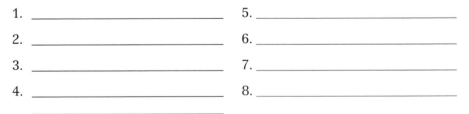

1. _____   5. _____

2. _____   6. _____

3. _____   7. _____

4. _____   8. _____

Uncontrollables include variables like: coach's decisions, teammates, crowd, officials/umpires/referees, opponents, weather conditions, equipment problems, travel delays, injuries and illnesses, academic demands, playing time, media, etc.

Controllables

The controllables are all of the factors you have complete or a great deal of control over. Take a minute to list the factors that you can control:

1. _____   5. _____

2. _____   6. _____

3. _____   7. _____

4. _____   8. _____

Controllables include variables like: attitude, effort, commitment, focus, confidence, diet, rest, responses to situations, communication, body language, coachability, preparation, etc.

To maintain your composure, the key is to properly identify what is a controllable and what is an uncontrollable. When you are in a difficult situation, ask yourself this simple question   Is it a controllable or uncontrollable?

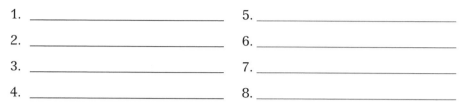

- If it is an uncontrollable, stop focusing on it and getting frustrated about it because there is nothing you can do anyway. You will need to ignore, work around, or adjust to it.

- If it is a controllable, you must take responsibility for controlling it and act!

Controlling the Controllables sounds simple—and it is. But most people have a hard time mentally breaking the habit of letting go of things that are outside of their control. Discipline yourself to focus on and take responsibility for the controllables, and you will be able to successfully control yourself.

3. Focus on the Present

Along with controlling the controllables, another effective strategy is to refocus yourself on the present moment. When you think about it, I'll bet that many of the times you experience yellows it is because you are frustrated by your past mistakes. How many times have you gotten frustrated with an early mistake you made (a missed shot, unforced error, turnover, etc.) and it ended up sticking with you for minutes, hours, and even days afterwards?

Many athletes have a hard time bouncing back from mistakes. Instead of moving on to the next play, you mentally get stuck in the past as you replay the mistake over and over again and get more and more frustrated with yourself. (This is especially true for those of you who are perfectionists.) You end up fighting yourself because a portion of your focus is still on the past. And if some of your focus is still on the past, it means that you are not 100% focused on the present.

- **Deep Breath**—The key then is the ability to mentally let go of the past and bring your mind back to the present moment. You can remind yourself to focus on the present moment by taking a deep breath and releasing past frustrations and distractions when you exhale.

- **Self Talk and Cue Words**—Then you can use your self talk (your internal dialogue with yourself) to focus on the present by saying, "Take care of this point," or "One point at a time," or "Focus right here, right now." Duke men's basketball coach Mike Krzyzewski uses the phrase "Next Play" with his team to remind his players that they need to forget about the past when they make mistakes and focus on the next play.

- **Learn a Lesson**—Another way of bringing your mind back to the present is to convert your mistakes, errors, and losses into lessons. Instead of dwelling on what you didn't do right last time, focus on the lesson you learned and how you plan to do it correctly the next time. Look to learn as much as you can about yourself, teammates, coaches, and opponents so you can apply that information to help you be successful in the future.

4. Focus on the Positive.

Picture this scenario: You walk into a fast food restaurant and decide to order a hamburger. The waiter asks for your order and you say, "I don't want a pizza, I don't want a taco, I don't want a salad, I don't want . . ." What would happen? Well, the waiter would probably get pretty frustrated and confused and finally say in an exasperated voice, "What DO you want?"

Similarly, sometimes athletes go into situations focused more on the negative mistakes they don't want to make rather than the positive plays they want to happen. How many times have you told yourself "Don't turn the ball over," "Don't miss!", or "Don't make a mistake"? When you focus on the negative mistakes you want to avoid your mind and body become confused and frustrated like the waiter did in the example. Instead, focus on the positive plays you want to make ("I want a hamburger") rather than the negative mistakes you want to avoid. Tell yourself, "Take care of the ball and make smart passes," "See the ball and drive it," and "I can make this play." By picturing and telling yourself about the positive plays you want to make, your mind can focus appropriately on making them happen.

5. Focus on the process.

Have you ever seen a team get excited and congratulate their teammate for making an out? Arizona Softball Coach Mike Candrea and his players congratulate teammates for outs when they hit the ball hard and the defense needs to make a great play to get them out. They do this because they understand that if you can continually focus on the process, the positive outcomes you want will take care of themselves. If the batter consistently makes solid contact with the ball, sooner or later she will get the desired outcome of a hit. By focusing on the process and doing the little things well, Arizona Softball has won numerous National Championships.

Keep in mind that the outcome of winning depends on your ability to focus on the process of competing. You must continually focus on doing the little things that will put you in a position to achieve the outcomes you want. What is the process of being successful in your sport? What will it take to achieve the outcomes you want? In most cases, focusing on the process involves taking care of the small yet important variables within your control—making a commitment to quality training, approaching situations with a great attitude, developing your physical and mental strengths, and working together with your teammates and coaches. By taking care of the process, you will put yourself in the best possible position to achieve the outcomes you want.

Show the Positive Emotions and Control the Negative

Finally, being composed doesn't mean you need to play like an emotionless robot. In essence, learning how to manage your emotions is what composure is all about. Feel free to show your positive emotions within reason. Celebrate your successes and those of your teammates—but not too much that you show up your opponents and provide them with an extra source of motivation. Positive emotion is critical in sport and it is often up to you as the leader to be the key catalyst.

WEEK 4

While it is good to show your positive emotions, do your best to keep your negative emotions in check. Sometimes this means disguising your frustration, or at least tempering it so that you don't lose control of yourself. If you can't control your own emotions, you will likely end up distracting many of your teammates. Your negative emotions could even infect them and start bringing them down as well. Therefore, be sure to practice the techniques we discussed in this chapter to make sure you can keep yourself, and your teammates, in the green light.

Chapter Four Summary

Your success as a leader depends on your ability to remain cool, calm, and collected under pressure. Recognize when you are beginning to get frustrated and refocus your mind back on to the controllables, the present, the positive, and the process. The key to composure is learning how to effectively manage your emotions.

KEY POINTS FROM CHAPTER FOUR

List three to five major points or insights you gained from this chapter:

1. _____

2. _____

3. _____

4. _____

5. _____

PRACTICAL EXERCISES FOR CHAPTER FOUR

1. Interview someone with a stressful job (ER doctor/nurse, air traffic controller, police officer, firefighter, sports official, another coach, etc.) Ask them:

- What are the most stressful situations for you?

_____

_____

- What do you do to maintain your composure during these times?

_____

_____

- What are the likely consequences if you let the pressure get to you?

_____

_____

2. Watch another team's practice or competition to observe them. During the practice/game watch to see what color lights the captains, coaches, and athletes seem to be in during various points in the competition.

- When was the coach in a green/yellow/red? How could you tell?

_____

_____

- When was the captain(s) in a green/yellow/red? How could you tell?

_____

_____

- What seemed to lead the team into yellows and reds?

_____

_____

- How did they handle these yellow and red light situations?

_____

_____

COACH/CAPTAIN MEETING NOTES

Next Meeting Date:
Time:

CHAPTER FIVE

CHARACTER

HOW TO CONDUCT YOURSELF WITH CLASS

*"Leadership is a potent combination of strategy and character. But if
you must be without one, be without the strategy."*
GENERAL H. NORMAN SCHWARZKOPF

Last but certainly not least, Leading by Example means that you are a
person of character. To earn the respect of your teammates and coaches,
you must be willing to consistently do the right thing—no matter what
the consequences. You must act with honesty and integrity. You must make
sure you abide by and even model the rules and standards of the team. And
you must show respect to your teammates and coaches.

Do the Right Thing

As a leader, your coaches and teammates count on you to do the right thing in
a variety of situations. They will expect you to know right from wrong and to
act accordingly. This doesn't mean that you need to be a perfect angel all of the
time and can never do anything wrong, but it does mean that you must hold
yourself accountable to a higher standard. You must recognize that what you
do is being watched by many. And you must understand that all of your actions
either reflect positively or negatively on the rest of the team.

1. In Your Sport

Doing the right thing means that you play with class. While winning is highly important to you because you are so committed, you also understand that winning the right way is what it is all about. Do not let yourself fall into the trap of believing that "winning is everything." Because it is not. If you win by cheating, circumventing rules, and compromising your integrity, you might win and gain some short-term satisfaction. But ultimately the victory will be hollow because you will always be haunted by knowing that you didn't win the right way. Whether you get caught or not is beside the point. When you play with class, you "win" even when you lose.

"Would I love to win a national championship? Absolutely!
And is it something I think about? Absolutely! But I won't do it at all costs.
I won't sell my soul to win a national championship."
RHONDA REVELLE, NEBRASKA SOFTBALL COACH

- **Play aggressively but not dirty.** As a leader, you will probably be one of the most aggressive players on your team. However, know where to draw the line between being competitive and being cheap. You will compete against teams and individuals who will intentionally play dirty in an effort to distract and intimidate you and your teammates. Rise to the occasion and compete rather than stooping to their level and being cheap. Maintain your focus on your game and let your actions speak louder than your words.

  Michael Jordan's Chicago Bulls did not become champions until they learned how not to get caught up in the "Bad Boy" tactics used by their rival, the Detroit Pistons. Despite players deliberately committing hard fouls on the Bulls in an effort to intimidate them, the Bulls went about their business and let their play do the talking on the court.

- **Respect officials.** Treat the referees, umpires, judges, and officials with respect. Of course there will be many times when the calls will go against you and your team. It is up to you to handle them with class and get yourself and your team focused on the next play. Leave the arguing of calls to your coaches if they so choose. Officials are human beings too. Treat them with respect in your pre-game conferences and when you interact with them during the competition. Being nice to them may not guarantee that you will get a call in your favor. But being a jerk to them certainly doesn't help your cause or reputation.

- **Obey the rules of the game, conference, association.** Be sure to know and play by the rules. Every week the sports pages are filled with the sad stories of athletes and coaches who think they are above the rules. Protect your eligibility always. Don't do stupid things like gambling or accepting extra benefits that are sure to jeopardize your eligibility and your team's chances of success. Ignorance is not an excuse, especially for leaders. If you are unsure about something, you are probably right not to do it. Talk to your coach or compliance officer to get a rules clarification. If you are afraid to ask about it, you probably shouldn't participate in it.

- **Watch your language.** Be careful about the language you use. This principle extends beyond "swear words" to derogatory racial comments, ethnic slurs, and comments about a person's sexual orientation. Not only are your teammates and coaches listening, but also many young and highly impressionable children. Whether you want to be or not, you are a role model to many children in your community; act accordingly.

- **Be a gracious winner and loser.** Win and lose with class. Be a model of good sportsmanship for your teammates. Celebrate your victories but not at the expense of your opponents. Do not rub it in their faces. You only serve to give them more motivation the next time you meet. When you lose, acknowledge your opponents, even if they might have won in less than ethical ways. Sooner or later, they will get what they deserve.

WEEK 5

How would you rate your commitment to doing the right thing in your sport?

_____

_____

_____

2. In the Classroom

Doing the right thing takes into account all the things you do outside of your sport. If you are a college or high school athlete, your academics will be an area where you are expected to lead. This doesn't mean that you need to have all A's. But it does mean that you must reasonably apply yourself, attend classes regularly, take good notes, and make a solid effort in the classroom. It means making your academics a priority and taking them seriously. It means being at least at the "compliant" if not "committed" level when it comes to your academics.

As a leader in the classroom, set the tone for your teammates; sit in the first three rows of class, get involved in class discussions, be a leader in group projects, let your professors know ahead of time when you might miss class because of travel and competitions, study on road trips, turn in your assignments on time, and, of course, do your own work. If your teammates see you hitting the books, they will be more likely to do the same.

How would you rate your commitment to doing the right thing in the class-room?

_____

_____

_____

3. In Your Social Life

Doing the right thing especially pertains to your social life. You certainly can and should have a social life. You need some kind of outlet to relax from all the pressures of your sport and school. However, you must keep your social life under control. The key to having a positive social life is balance and moderation. You will need to balance your social time with your athletic and academic obligations. In season, your social life will often need to rank third behind your academic and athletic responsibilities. If your social life ranks first, you will have an extremely difficult time gaining the respect of your coaches and teammates.

Doing the right thing in your social life takes into account your use of alcohol and/or other drugs. As a leader, you determine the kind of environment that is acceptable. If you are out abusing alcohol and other drugs, then other people on the team (especially the freshmen) are much more likely to do the same. However, if you avoid using alcohol, or if you are of age and drink responsibly, you set a great example for the rest of your teammates to follow. You can be a Leader by Example or a Vocal Leader when it comes to your teammates' alcohol-related behavior. The same holds true for your sexual behavior. Be sure to respect yourself and others. You can very quickly lose respect and develop an unwanted reputation if you're not careful. The bad reputation of just a couple members of your team can cause your entire team to be seen in a negative light and not be taken seriously. Conduct yourself with class and insist that your teammates do the same.

How would you rate your commitment to doing the right thing in your social life?

_____

_____

_____

What role do alcohol and other drugs play in your life?

_____

_____

_____

4. In the Community

Finally, doing the right thing also relates to your involvement in your community. Many teams find ways to give back to their communities via speaking at schools, volunteering at homeless shelters, working for Habitat for Humanity, and a variety of other community service projects. Not only is volunteering the right thing to do, but it also projects a positive image of your team in the community. As a leader, take the initiative to seek out these opportunities. Get your teammates involved and excited about doing them. Community service often is a great team building activity. Giving to others is a win/win situation for them and your team as you realize how fortunate you are to be an athlete.

College athletes should contact their Life Skills Coordinator and high school students can contact their guidance counselors to find out more about the wealth of community service activities that are available in your community.

How would you rate your commitment to doing the right thing in your community?

_____

_____

_____

WEEK 5

Knowing Right from Wrong

How can you tell the difference between right and wrong? There are a lot of gray areas in sport and in life. While your team likely has a series of rules that you are expected to follow, it can't cover everything. Even as thick as the NCAA Rulebook is, there are always going to be some situations which arise that are not specifically covered by the rules.

As a leader, you will be expected to know and do the right thing. Here are two simple tests you can use if you ever have difficulty deciding what the right thing to do might be.

Social Media Test

Imagine if what you are thinking about doing (or not doing) were posted across all of your social media sites. For example, Joe Athlete Lets Teammate Drive Drunk, Sue Athlete Cheats on History Test, Jim Athlete Cheapshots Opponent. If the potential posts would cause you, your team, and/or your coach any embarrassment, then you probably have your answer.

Proud to Tell Mom or Dad Test

Another simple test would be to imagine having to tell your mom or dad what you have done. If you don't think they would be proud of your decision, then you likely have the right answer as well.

Honesty Is the Best Policy

Being a person of character also means you are honest and trustworthy. You must be willing to tell the truth when others ask for it or need to hear it, rather than running away from it because you are scared or uncomfortable. Remember that people may not always like to hear the truth, but they will appreciate your honesty. Certainly there will be times when you need to be tactful and sugar-coat your words a little bit to preserve a person's confidence. However, you ultimately do people a disservice in the long run if you aren't willing to be honest with them.

Abide by the Rules

If you expect your teammates to follow the team's rules and standards, be sure that you are modeling them first. It is critical that you are early or, at the worst, on time for practices, travel, and team functions. Be sure you turn in your uniform when it is needed and follow through with your team obligations. Do what you say you are going to do. And do what other people need and expect you to do.

Respect Others

Be a good sport by showing respect to everyone. Whether it is your coach, teammates, managers, parents, trainers, teachers/professors, fans, and yes even your opponents, give people the respect they deserve. These people will probably not always treat you with respect, but as a leader it is up to you to be the "bigger" person. Be courteous and respectful. Say "please" and "thank you." In the long run, the vast majority of people will forget all of your individual stats and your team's win/loss records, but they will remember whether or not you treated them with class.

Finally, respecting others means that you refuse to bad mouth people behind their backs. This is an easy temptation to fall into because it seems like someone is always having some kind of frustration with a coach or teammate. However, as a leader, not only must you avoid starting gossip about your teammates (and coaches), but you must also stop it in its tracks when you hear it.

Chapter Five Summary

Your character is critical as a Leader by Example. You won't always be perfect; but do your best to do the right thing whether you are on the field, in the classroom, or in the community. Represent yourself, your family, your team, and your school with pride and class and you will win the respect of many.

KEY POINTS FROM CHAPTER FIVE

List three to five major points or insights you gained from this chapter:

1. _____

2. _____

3. _____

4. _____

5. _____

PRACTICAL EXERCISES FOR CHAPTER FIVE

1. Interview a leader who you feel has tremendous integrity (principal, athletic director, school president, teacher/professor, CEO of a company, etc.). Ask them:

WEEK
5

- What kind of ethical decisions must you make on a regular basis?

_____

_____

_____

- What guidelines do you use to help you make ethical decisions?

_____

_____

_____

- What problems have you seen when people act without conscience?

_____

_____

_____

- What advice do you have for me as a leader when it comes to character and integrity?

_____

_____

_____

2. Organize a community service event for your team. You can read at a local school, work on a house for Habitat for Humanity, volunteer at a soup kitchen, run a mini-clinic for your community's recreation department, clean up a neighborhood park, volunteer for Special Olympics, visit a nursing home, Ronald McDonald House, or hospital, etc. The time invested will produce a win/win experience for everyone.

COMPANION ONLINE LEADERSHIP RESOURCE

For more information,
visit www.TeamCaptainsNetwork.com

COACH/CAPTAIN MEETING NOTES

_____

_____

_____

_____

_____

_____

_____

_____

_____

_____

_____

_____

_____

_____

_____

_____

_____

_____

_____

_____

_____

_____

_____

_____

_____

WEEK 5

Next Meeting Date:
Time:

HOW TO BE A VOCAL LEADER

"Vocal leadership is calculated instruction, encouragement, or whatever the team may need at precisely the right time and in the right tone of voice."
LAUREN GREGG, U.S. SOCCER NATIONAL TEAM ASSISTANT COACH

As we discussed in Section One, leadership begins with the ability to lead yourself first. That's why the first part of *The Team Captain's Leadership Manual* focused on the skills you need to be able to lead yourself effectively. As you probably realize, leading yourself effectively is a big enough challenge all by itself. You have to be able to develop and master the Leading by Example component of leadership to make sure that you can walk your talk and earn your coaches' respect and teammates' trust. No one will follow a leader who preaches one thing but practices another. Once you understand what it means to lead yourself and develop the skills to do it effectively, the even greater challenge is to master the art of Vocal Leadership.

WEEK
6

Not only can Vocal Leaders lead themselves effectively, but they also have the people skills necessary to effectively lead others. Being a Vocal Leader is especially challenging because now you must have the people skills to deal with a variety of personalities, backgrounds, and races that all combine to make a team. What motivates, refocuses, and calms one person might be the exact opposite of what you would need to do with a different person. You must develop an effective relationship with each of your teammates which will take time and initiative on your part. The second part of this manual focuses on the skills you will need to develop and hone to lead your teammates as a Vocal Leader.

A Vocal Leader Must Emerge

Why are Vocal Leaders so important? Because so many situations, challenges, conflicts, and problems occur throughout the season that require someone to step up, speak up, and deal with them with assertiveness and tact. Leaders by Example are certainly valuable and important people to have on a team, but in reality, they are often not enough. If a person chooses only to Lead by Example and not get involved verbally, they aren't able to adequately address many of the issues that effective team leadership requires. At least one of the Leaders by Example will need to go the critical next step and evolve into a Vocal Leader.

Transforming Leaders by Example into Vocal Leaders

Why do some athletes make the jump from Leader by Example to Vocal Leader? Here are three typical reasons:

1. Sometimes people are more apt to be Vocal Leaders because of their personality and communication skills. Some people are more extroverted/outgoing and comfortable communicating with others. They are natural communicators and feel that it would be virtually impossible to lead without communicating.

2. Other athletes emerge as Vocal Leaders as they become more established on the team. When they are young, many athletes feel it is not their place to speak out so they defer to the veterans on the team. They feel like they might be stepping on the toes of the more experienced athletes on the team if they try to speak out. Basically, they lack the confidence necessary to step forward and lead. As they become more established on the team, they feel they have more of a right and responsibility to be a leader.

3. Finally some of the more shy and reserved Leaders by Example become Vocal Leaders because of their competitiveness and commitment. Normally quiet, many highly competitive athletes can get so frustrated when things are going wrong that they can't help but speak up and become Vocal Leaders. They care so much about the team's success that they step outside of their normal comfort zone and are willing to speak up for the good of the team.

Ultimately, a person's level of communication skills, confidence, competitiveness, and commitment are the primary reasons why some people emerge as Vocal Leaders. Remember, your team must have one person who is willing to step outside of themselves to be a Vocal Leader. Are you that person?

Who is going to step up and be a Vocal Leader for your team?

_____

_____

_____

What do you need to do to become a more Vocal Leader?

_____

_____

_____

Communication Skills are Critical

The key to being an effective Vocal Leader revolves around your ability to listen and communicate effectively. Ironically, listening is actually the first step of being a good Vocal Leader.

First Listen Up . . .

You must truly listen to your teammates to know where they are coming from, what motivates them, and what frustrates them. The only way you can do this is to listen to them. Once you get to know each of your teammates and develop a solid relationship with them, then and only then can you begin to communicate with them more effectively. You will have a better feel for what to say, how to say it, when to say it, and why you are saying it. Look to listen first and communicate second.

Then Speak Up

Being a Vocal Leader means just that—you must communicate. During practices and games, your voice should be heard just as much as your coaches, sometimes more so. You must communicate clearly and frequently with your teammates. You are not communicating just to talk. You are communicating to build confidence, keep the team focused, confront problems, stay in touch with coaches, and show your teammates that you care about them and the team.

There are numerous opportunities to communicate every day and it is important to take advantage of them. This means talking with teammates before practice to check in with them. It means getting them energized and focused for the practice. It means verbally complimenting their successes and appreciating their efforts. It means challenging them when their efforts or performance fall below expectations. It means refocusing them when they become frustrated and distracted. It means talking with them about their academics and social life when they go astray. Again, a lot of feeling comfortable about speaking up goes back to having confidence in yourself.

WEEK 6

The Two Primary Roles of Vocal Leaders

As a Vocal Leader, there are two primary roles that you will need to play; you will need to be both an Encourager and Enforcer with your teammates. Below is a general overview of each role and the subsequent chapters will give you detailed information and tips for fulfilling each role.

1. Encourager

As the name suggests, the role of Encourager is to inspire, support, and refocus your teammates through the ups (greens) and downs (yellows/reds) they are going to have throughout the course of your season. It is your job to help them feel comfortable, play with confidence, find optimism when they face obstacles, and keep them focused despite the many distractions they will have both on and off the playing field. As an Encourager, in many ways you have to be the mental game catalyst for your teammates. You have to create an environment that fosters green lights for them. You have to help them feel good about themselves because a good percentage of your teammates have a difficult time doing that on their own. Further, you have to be their life vest of hope when they are drowning in frustration, fear, and failure. You have to help refocus them when they are in yellows and reds—again because many of them have not adequately developed their own mental toughness to be able to do it on their own. You have to have your stuff together and try to help others do the same.

Being an Encourager is your primary job as a Vocal Leader. This Encouraging role has a variety of responsibilities associated with it including these four:

1. Being a Servant Leader to your teammates—Chapter Six

2. Being a Confidence-Builder for your teammates—Chapter Seven

3. Refocusing teammates when they struggle—Chapter Eight

4. Building your team's chemistry—Chapter Nine

2. Enforcer

As a leader, it is also up to you to establish, maintain, and enforce the rules, standards, and chemistry of your team. You must hold yourself and your teammates accountable. When teammates act in ways that are hurting themselves and the team, you have to be willing to constructively confront them. This means you must confront people when they are slacking off, cutting classes, gossiping about teammates, complaining about coaches, abusing their bodies, and any time when they are not living up to the rules and standards of the team. They must be made aware that the negative effects of their behavior are hurting the team and will not be tolerated.

Many leaders have a tough time addressing conflict because they are so uncomfortable with it. It is much easier to avoid or ignore dealing with these difficult issues in hopes that they will take care of themselves. Sometimes they do—but more often than not, they end up festering and mushrooming into full blown crises and major dramas that can distract, divide, and destroy your team. You must be on the lookout for little brush fires that you can control and douse while they are still in the early stages, because they have the potential to rage into damaging infernos if left unchecked. Clearly, the Enforcing role is not a fun or easy job, but one that must be done if you are going to be an effective Vocal Leader and have a successful team. Chapter 10 provides you with several helpful suggestions and strategies to help you be an effective Enforcer for your team.

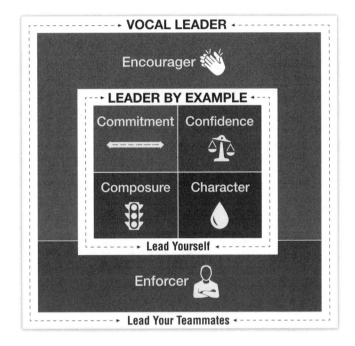

WEEK
6

ENCOURAGER—SERVANT LEADER

HOW TO PUT YOUR TEAMMATES FIRST

"Serve first, lead second."
ROBERT K. GREENLEAF, AUTHOR OF *SERVANT LEADERSHIP*

What Is Your Philosophy of Leadership?

Emily and Beth were voted co-captains by their teammates. Upon hearing the news, Emily began to think of what it meant to be a good leader. Most of the leaders Emily had observed growing up were very demanding and controlling people with an elitist attitude. They had a leadership philosophy that leaders needed to be in charge, be tough, and have a "my way or the highway" mentality. They also believed the leader had an elevated status among the team and it was up to the others to serve the leader.

Being exposed to this philosophy of leadership, Emily thought she should lead in the very same way. So she went to practice that afternoon and began ruling with an iron fist. "I'm leading the warmup today and I don't want to see any slacking off from the rest of you," she growled. Her teammates were a little surprised about her aggressive approach but let it go for now. After the warmup, Emily turned to one of the freshmen and said, "Hey freshman, go get my water bottle." Some of her teammates began thinking, "Who does she think she is? She shouldn't be ordering us around like that."

She continued being demanding of her teammates, especially the freshmen—expecting them to jump at her every command. At one point, one of the players made a couple of mistakes in a row and Emily let her have it in front of everyone. "Julie, I can't believe you can't make that play. There is no way we are ever going to be any good as a team if you keep playing like that. Either pick it up or go home." Julie was on the verge of tears and the rest of the team was stunned . . . Emily was definitely on a power trip because that's what she thought it meant to be a good leader.

Beth, on the other hand, had a different view of leadership. Beth had grown up with leaders who always seemed to put her needs ahead of their own. They looked to make Beth feel comfortable as a team member by taking her under their wing. They complimented her when she succeeded and they supported her when she struggled. They looked to make her life easier whenever they could. Beth felt like the leaders she had been around really cared about her and her success—and that they would do anything to help her be successful.

When Beth went to practice, she made sure to greet each of her teammates and sincerely ask how their day was going. After the warmup, she grabbed a bunch of water bottles for her teammates and then went back for her own. She brought an upbeat attitude to the drills and complimented several teammates for their good play and effort. When one of her teammates struggled, she took her to the side and reminded her to keep her head up. She gave her a quick tip and refocused her teammate. Beth believed good leadership was about putting others first and helping them feel good about themselves.

What do you think happened after practice? Of course, most of the team was fed up with what a jerk Emily had been at practice. If they knew she was going to act this way after being voted captain, they would have never given her a single vote. Emily and Beth obviously had a very different philosophy of what it meant to be an effective leader. They went about executing their leadership philosophies for another day before the problem came to a head. The teammates went to Beth to express the problems they were having with Emily. Beth tried to approach Emily about the effects of her demanding behavior but Emily let her have it, too. Finally Beth decided to talk with her coach about the situation. After a team meeting to sort things out, it was decided that Emily would lose the privilege of being captain. In just two short days, Emily lost the confidence, trust, and respect of her teammates. After reading through this true story, here are a few questions for you to think about and answer:

What kind of leadership styles were you exposed to over the years—parents, coaches, teachers, captains, others?

_____

_____

_____

What did you learn from these people about effective and ineffective leadership?

_____

_____

_____

_____

What is your philosophy of leadership all about?

_____

_____

_____

_____

Be a Servant Leader, Not a Self-serving Leader

Ultimately, you will find that serving others and putting their needs first is the best form of leadership. Called Servant Leadership by Robert Greenleaf, effective leaders make the team's needs the priority. It's more about your team's success, rather than your own individual success. When you look to help others feel good about themselves and succeed, the entire team benefits. But, if you think that leadership is all about others serving you and obeying your commands, your teammates will quickly come to fear and resent you rather than follow and respect you. Leaders seek to humbly serve others.

WEEK 6

"Team sports are usually difficult things. Sometimes your team wins because of you, sometimes in spite of you, and sometimes it's like you are not even there. That's the reality of the team game. Then at one point in my career, something wonderful happened. I don't know why or how, but I came to understand what a 'team' meant. It meant that although I didn't get a hit or make a great defensive play, I could impact the team in an incredible and consistent way. I could impact my team by caring first and foremost about the team's success and not my own. I don't mean rooting for us like a typical fan, fans are fickle. I mean care, really care about the team . . . about 'us.' I became less selfish, less lazy, less sensitive to negative comments. When I gave up me I became more. I became a captain, a leader, a better person and I came to understand that life is a team game. . . . And you know what? . . . I've found most people aren't team players. They don't realize that life is the only game in town. Someone should tell them. It has made all the difference in the world to me."

DON MATTINGLY, NEW YORK YANKEES FORMER CAPTAIN

Do the Grunt Work

Doing the Grunt Work might sound like a radical concept for some of you but it clearly shows you want to be a Servant Leader. Instead of giving the freshmen/ newcomers all of the tough jobs no one else wants to do, you can demonstrate you are a Servant Leader by jumping in and doing the chores yourself. It's the little things like cleaning up the locker room, sweeping the floor, raking the field, carrying the equipment, making sure the bus is clean, and other tedious but necessary jobs that show you are willing to serve your team. When your teammates see you as the leader taking care of these tasks, they will be more likely to pitch in and follow in your footsteps. Instead of thinking you are above them, you show them you are willing to do whatever it takes to help the team be successful.

"As quarterback of my team, I know people are looking to me for direction, guidance and leadership, so I set the best example I can. Everybody wants to be great, but that takes work, and I would never ask my teammates to do something I'm not willing to do myself. They know I'll be the first one at practice and the last to leave."

DREW BREES, NEW ORLEANS SAINTS

Take the Youngsters "Under Your Wing"

Being an Encourager means looking out for your teammates, especially the less experienced ones. Instead of getting frustrated with the freshmen, reach out to them and bring them into the fold. You must remember what it was like when you were a freshmen and/or new to the team. Most newcomers experience uncertainty about what is expected, worry about proving themselves, fear about fitting in, and sadness over missing friends and family from home. As a leader you should reach out to your teammates and offer yourself as a help to them during these tough times. Here are some simple actions that you can take to help them feel more welcome:

- If you are in college, ask to host recruits on their campus visits. It is never too early to start reaching out to your prospective teammates.

- Call or text new team members before they arrive to welcome them and offer your support.

- Put up a sign welcoming them to the team.

- Help them move in and get settled.

- Give them a school/campus tour so they know their way around.

- Make a guide book of the best restaurants, movie theaters, coffee houses, barber shops/hair salons, ATMs, laundromats, etc.

- Have them over for dinner.

- Read them the Dr. Seuss book *Oh, the Places You'll Go*— you'll get a lot out of it yourself, too!

A Word About Hazing: Why Not Help Instead of Humiliate Your Teammates?

Unfortunately, instead of helping their teammates feel more comfortable and confident when they come to campus, some leaders and teams choose to make their new teammates' lives even more miserable by initiating them with embarrassing pranks. They use peer pressure in forcing their teammates to drink excessively, wear bizarre clothing, and do a whole host of other stressful activities. Often called hazing, this archaic practice only serves to alienate and humiliate your teammates. It is more likely to hurt your team's chemistry than to help it. As a leader, why not look to help your new teammates feel like they are a part of the team rather than humiliate them? I've included several ideas in Chapter Nine on Team Building which are a lot more fun and effective team builders so check them out as a great and productive alternative to hazing.

If I Knew Then What I Know Now

Good team leaders also invest the time to share helpful suggestions and strategies with their younger teammates that they might have learned the hard way. Let your teammates know about some of the challenges you and your fellow veteran teammates endured when you were younger. Warn your freshman about some of the typical pitfalls, obstacles, and setbacks they are likely to face their freshman year: homesickness, relationships, grades, drinking, sitting the bench, etc. Talk about any struggles you might have had and, most importantly, what you learned from them. Give them tips and strategies to avoid or minimize the problems as much as possible. And when they do stumble, make sure you are there for them for support and encouragement. (For more success tips on surviving and thriving as a college student-athlete, check out the book *If I Knew Then What I Know Now* by Becky Bell.)

WEEK 6

---

*"All the guys on my team, they know if they need anything
all they've gotta do is pick up the phone, I'm going to be there for them
to support them any way I can."*

LARRY FITZGERALD, ARIZONA CARDINALS

Keep Tabs on Your Teammates

Encouragers invest the time to check in with their teammates to see how they are doing. Make a point to be accessible to your teammates. Be sure to touch base with each of them on a regular basis. Ask them how they are doing, how their classes are going, what their families are up to, etc. Show your teammates that you care about them, but also be sure not to be too overbearing. Obviously you don't want it to seem like you are prying too much into their personal lives or spying on them. But you do want to show an interest in each of your teammates and provide them with an opportunity to open up more with you if they want to. Should something be troubling them, you hope they would feel comfortable enough to talk with you about it. Remember that trust must be built over time so be patient. Here are some tips to keep in mind when a teammate comes to you with a concern.

1. Listen Before You Leap

When a teammate does come to you with a problem, focus first on listening and understanding rather than trying to fix the problem for them. Sometimes all you need to do is to listen so your teammates can vent their frustrations and sort out their thoughts. Just talking about it and getting it out in the open is often enough to get the person back on track.

2. Explore Options and Consequences

Once you listen to them and understand the situation correctly, you can then help them explore some of the options they might have. If you have had experience with what they are going through, you can share your stories of both what worked and what didn't work in an effort to help them learn from your experience.

3. Follow Up

Check back with them to see how they are doing. Following up in a timely manner shows that you care about them enough to see if they have resolved their problem.

Tips for Good Listening

- **Eliminate Distractions**—Turn off your cell phone and give your teammate your full attention.

- **Eye Contact**—One of the best ways to demonstrate you are listening is to make good eye contact.

- **Nodding and Affirming**—Use small gestures and phrases to show you are really listening. You can nod your head in agreement, raise your eyebrows for surprise, use touch for support. You can also use short phrases like "yes, sure, I understand, really" etc. as you listen attentively.

- **Don't Interrupt**—Give them a chance to present their side of the story without interrupting.

- **Tune Into Their Body Language**—Hear what is being said but also tune into what they might be communicating to you with their body language. It often reveals more than the words that are spoken.

- **Paraphrase**—From time to time, rephrase what you heard them say in your own words to check to see if you understand them correctly.

  "What I heard you say was . . ."

  "So what you are saying is . . ."

  "Let me get this straight . . ."

- **Empathize**—Empathizing is a special kind of paraphrasing where you look to reflect back the feelings the other person is experiencing.

  "That sounds like it is really *frustrating* for you . . ."

  "You must be really *angry* about that . . ."

  "It seems like you are *upset* about the situation . . ."

Take Care of Yourself, Too

Yes, servant leadership is about taking care of others—but not at the expense of yourself. Be careful not to get overextended in helping others that you neglect yourself in the process. If your game or health is suffering because you always feel exhausted, stressed out, and overwhelmed, you won't be effective for yourself or anyone else. You must keep up your strength, energy, and enthusiasm so that you can transfer it to others. Invest the time to eat well, get enough rest and relaxation, and recharge your batteries whenever possible—you and your team will be glad you did.

WEEK 6

Chapter Six Summary

Basically, being a Servant Leader means that you truly care about your teammates. You want what is best for them both on and off the court, field, track, etc. And you willingly demonstrate your concern for them by reaching out, passing on experiences, and being there for them as a resource and a source of support when they make mistakes. Investing the time to take care of your teammates will certainly pay off for them. But it will also pay off for you, too, as you will have teammates who will not only want to win for themselves—but for you as well.

KEY POINTS FROM CHAPTER SIX

List three to five major points or insights you gained from this chapter:

1. _____

2. _____

3. _____

4. _____

5. _____

PRACTICAL ACTIVITIES FOR CHAPTER SIX

1. Ask five veteran athletes about some of the most important lessons they learned.

- What are the three most important pieces of advice you would give to a newcomer about succeeding in your sport?

  _____

  _____

  _____

- What are the three most important pieces of advice you would give to a newcomer about succeeding in school?

  _____

  _____

  _____

- What are the three most important pieces of advice you would give to a newcomer about succeeding socially?

  _____

  _____

  _____

- What tips do you have for successfully balancing all of these different areas?

  _____

  _____

  _____

Compile these responses and share them with your newcomers.

COMPANION ONLINE LEADERSHIP RESOURCE

For more information,
visit www.TeamCaptainsNetwork.com

COACH/CAPTAIN MEETING NOTES

WEEK 6

Next Meeting Date:
Time:

CHAPTER SEVEN

ENCOURAGER—CONFIDENCE-BUILDER

HOW TO INSPIRE YOUR TEAMMATES

"A good leader inspires people to have confidence in the leader, a great leader inspires people to have confidence in themselves."
LAO TZU

WEEK
7

Being an Encourager means that you are also a Confidence-Builder for your teammates. As we discussed in the Confidence section earlier, confidence is very fragile for many athletes as it fluctuates up and down throughout the season. Because your teammates' confidence will not always be where it should be, you will have to provide a great deal of encouragement and stability for them.

Each of your teammates will be somewhat different in regard to their confidence. Some of them will be pretty solid and stable while others will lose their confidence in a matter of seconds.

Develop a Relationship with Each Teammate

As a Vocal Leader, you must develop a working relationship with each of your teammates. You need to invest the time to get to know each of your teammates so you know how to best communicate with them. You must understand both what fires them up and what frustrates them. You will naturally know some of your teammates well because you have similar interests or you have already spent a lot of time together and you have seen them in a variety of situations. Others, like the newcomers and the people you don't normally hang out with, are people who you will need to make a conscious effort to get to know better.

"Being a leader, you have to be able to find some things in common with all the guys. Sometimes, maybe on the surface, you'll look at another guy and think you don't really have anything in common with him, so that's when you have to make the extra effort to get to know that guy. Find out what makes him tick. And that's when you find that you do have something in common with him."
JASON GIAMBI, NEW YORK YANKEES

As the setter and co-captain for her college volleyball team, Dana was focused on winning a national championship. She and Sarah, the team's outside hitter, were both juniors and had developed a great connection between them. Dana knew where Sarah was going to be and vice versa. With Dana and Sarah leading the way, the team had a spectacular season and had advanced to the NCAA Regional Finals where they were playing the number one ranked team for the chance to make it to the Final Four. Dana and Sarah were really clicking early, leading the team to a first game win. They came out strong again in the second game as they were up by six late and ready to take control of the match.

As Sarah planted to go up for yet another kill, she severely twisted her ankle and had to be taken out for the rest of the match. Of course, Dana was stunned at first but she tried to refocus herself and her team for the rest of the match.

The person who subbed in for Sarah was a sophomore named Heidi. Heidi had played sparingly throughout the season but the team really depended on her now. Dana wanted to try to make Heidi feel comfortable and confident in this difficult situation, but she didn't really know what to say to her. Because she didn't think Heidi would ever play much, Dana never made the effort to get to know her during the season. They rarely warmed up together and Dana never spent any time with Heidi outside of the locker room. On the court, it was evident the two were struggling to connect. The momentum of the match turned quickly as Dana and the rest of her teammates became more and more frustrated. The number one ranked team got back into the match quickly and went on to win in four games.

After the match, Dana's biggest regret was not investing the time to get to know each of her teammates. Even though Sarah had gone down at a critical time, Dana knew that if she and Heidi had just connected a little bit more, the team could have won and advanced to the Final Four.

"Almost everything in leadership comes back to relationships. The only way you can possibly lead people is to understand people. And the best way to do that is to get to know them better."
MIKE KRZYZEWSKI, DUKE MEN'S BASKETBALL

Take a Mental Game Assessment of each Teammate

To help you get to know each teammate better, I strongly recommend that you do a Mental Game Assessment of each one. Write the names of each teammate in a notebook. Below each name, write down your answers to the following 10 questions for each teammate.

TEAMMATE MENTAL GAME ASSESSMENT

Name: _____

- What motivates him/her?

- How confident is he/she? Why?

- How does he/she handle pressure situations and adversity?

- When does he/she tend to get frustrated, down, and angry?

- What can I do/say when he/she is struggling to help get him/her back on track?

- Who does he/she trust the most/least on the team?

- How does he/she feel about his/her role on the team?

- How is his/her relationship with the coaches?

- How would I describe my relationship with him/her?

- What are his/her biggest strengths (physically and mentally)?

- What are his/her biggest weaknesses (physically and mentally)?

WEEK 7

You may feel pretty confident about your answers to these questions for some of your teammates, but others you may struggle with for now. That's okay. It's your job to recognize which teammates you might not know as well and begin developing a stronger relationship with each of them. Then, roughly a month from now when you come back to this assessment, you will have a much better feel for each of your teammates. The answers to these questions provide valuable insights on how you should communicate with each of your teammates. **Of course, you will want to keep this list highly confidential.**

(**Author's Note:** *If you have a large team as in football or even baseball, you can divide up your teammates between yourselves if you have more than one captain/team leader. Each of you can take the primary responsibility for getting to know certain teammates.*)

Combine Your Insights with Your Coach's

After completing your list, I highly recommend that you have your coach(es) complete the assessment of each of your teammates as well. Then sit down with your coach in a private meeting and compare and discuss your answers for each teammate. Combining your ideas with your coach's should give you a more accurate read on each teammate. Remember that you are doing this exercise to gain a better understanding of each teammate, not to criticize them. This background information should help you know how to lead each of them through a variety of situations. If you and your coach are not sure about the answers to some of the questions, you have a couple of options:

1. Be more observant of the person over the next few weeks to see if you can figure out the answer to the question(s) you are unsure of.

2. You can simply ask your teammates about anything you are unsure of. You can let them know that as a captain, you want to get to know them better so you can help them play at their best. You can ask them what are the best ways you can motivate them to consistently perform up to their potential.

Armed with the insights from the Teammate Mental Game Assessment, you will have a better feel for how you might best approach each teammate no matter what the situation. As a Vocal Leader, you will have to pay particular attention to your teammates who struggle with their confidence, have a tendency to choke under pressure, get frustrated with themselves, have difficulty accepting their role, and have a strained relationship with coaches or other teammates. It is important for you to keep good tabs on them.

How to Motivate Your Teammates by Building Their Confidence

As a Vocal Leader, not only do you have to pump yourself up to perform, but you also need to make sure your teammates are in a confident mindset. Some of your teammates will be able to do this on their own. Others you will need to monitor and assist from time to time. Still others you may have to dedicate a lot of attention to because of their lack of confidence. After doing the Teammate Mental Game Assessment, you should have a better feel for which teammates tend to be more fragile when it comes to their confidence.

Check in with these people to see if they need a confidence boost every now and then. Use the suggestions below to eventually teach them how to create confidence on their own, without always relying on you to do it for them.

1. Accentuate the Positive and the Progress

Call attention to the positive strides your teammates make. You need to not only acknowledge the successes they have but also the effort they display. One of the best ways to do this is to use the phrase, "I see you . . ." For example, "I see you working hard in the weight room. That's going to pay off for you and this team." Or, "I see you making the extra effort on that play. . . . Keep doing that and you'll get it next time." Vocal Leaders help their teammates feel good about themselves by acknowledging and emphasizing the positive.

"Great leaders inflate the people around them.
Poor leaders deflate the people around them."
RICK PITINO, LOUISVILLE MEN'S BASKETBALL

2. Let Them Know What to Expect

Many people lack confidence because they aren't sure what to expect when they head into new situations. Your job as a leader is to quell their uncertainty and confusion when possible. Thus, you can let your new teammates know what to expect in terms of practices, school, travel, tournaments, playoffs, etc.

For example, because many Olympic athletes have never competed at some of the venues prior to the Olympic games, some coaches will have someone videotape the competition area ahead of time to show to the athletes. They also video the Olympic village, dormitory, cafeteria, buses, etc. in an effort to help their athletes know what to expect. Similarly, give your teammates a preview of what is to come in an effort to help them feel more comfortable and confident.

3. Remind Them of Their Strengths

As we discussed in the Confidence section earlier, helping people focus on their strengths is a great way to help them be more confident. Using the Teammate Mental Game Assessment you completed earlier, remind your teammates about the individual strengths they bring to the team. For example, "Greg, you are one of this team's best defenders because of your quickness and anticipation. Get in there and shut him down." Or, "Cammie, there is no one in this conference who has a better change-up than you do—use it to your advantage." Strangely, your teammates often forget about what they do best when competition rolls around. It's your job to remind them where they excel and to encourage them to go to battle with it.

4. Remind Them of Their Past Successes

If a teammate is starting to tense up in a tight situation, remind them of past similar situations where they came through for the team. "Hey Paul, this is just like last year when we were down 14 points going into the fourth quarter against State University. We did it then so let's do it again." Or, "Wendi, remember the time your freshman year when you hit two free throws with no time on the clock to send the game into overtime? You are money." Reminding people of their past successes provides them with a tangible example of their ability to be successful. Help them feel like they can do it again because they have already proven they could do it in the past.

5. Remind Them of Their Preparation and Hard Work

Finally, you need to remind your teammates that they deserve to be successful because of all the preparation and work they have already invested. Remind them that they have paid the price of success through their training, weight lifting, conditioning, diet, etc. You must convince them that they have worked just as hard, if not harder, than your opponents. In that way, they should feel like they deserve to be successful because they have done more. "Ryan, no one has worked harder on their game than you have. How many people were up at 6:00 a.m. every morning working their tail off like you were? It's in there. Trust yourself." Or, "Jill, you are more than ready. Now is the time all of that conditioning, weight lifting, and agilities will pay off."

6. "Just-ify" Their Thinking

Another way to help your teammates feel confident is to remind them to keep the game simple. Too many athletes have a tendency to overcomplicate the game and put too much pressure on themselves to perform. Help them keep it simple by something I call "just-ifying" their thinking.

For example, I once asked Alison Johnsen-McCutcheon, college softball's all-time career hits leader, what she thought about as she stepped into the batter's box to hit. She said, "I simply told myself, '*Just* put a good swing on a good pitch.'" By using the word "just" she mentally transformed the complex process of hitting a ball that is coming at 60 mph and moving in a variety of directions into a simple task she could do. Keeping it simple kept her confident. Similarly, some golfers will remind themselves to "*just* put a good roll on it" when they are putting. Encourage your teammates to keep it simple by "just-ifying" their thinking.

7. Show and Tell Teammates You Believe in Them

Let your teammates know you have confidence in them. Because of your leadership position and the respect you have earned, they will be highly likely to listen and respond to you. Tell your teammates you believe in them. By demonstrating your confidence in your teammates through your words, body language, and actions, you can positively and profoundly affect their confidence.

Admittedly, sometimes it's tough to tell your teammates you have confidence in them when in reality you have your doubts. While you don't want to lie to them, you also don't want them to sense that you don't believe in them. Sometimes they need you to show them more confidence than you actually feel. People will often perform up to your expectations as long as you give them the proper support and encouragement.

Chapter Seven Summary

Ultimately building confidence in your teammates is all about reminding them why they deserve to be successful. You must focus them on the strengths they have going for them and help them minimize their doubts and fears. Keep the game simple and manageable. Help them get their minds in a position where they can be successful.

"You have to understand the strengths of the people you are working with. Everybody on your team has a role, and each role is as important as the other... Everybody has strengths and weaknesses, and what you try to do is put everybody in the best position to succeed by utilizing their strengths."
DREW BREES, NEW ORLEANS SAINTS

"You have to keep talking to them and encouraging them. I think you really have to know each player and how to get to them, how to get them fired up."
CARLA OVERBECK, U.S. NATIONAL SOCCER TEAM

KEY POINTS FROM CHAPTER SEVEN

WEEK
7

List three to five major points or insights you gained from this chapter:

1. _____

2. _____

3. _____

4. _____

5. _____

PRACTICAL EXERCISES FOR CHAPTER SEVEN

1. Interview a counselor, coach, minister, or another helping professional. Ask them:

- What role does confidence play in the people you work with?

  _____

  _____

  _____

- Why do some people seem to lack confidence?

  _____

  _____

  _____

- What do you do to build confidence in others?

  _____

  _____

  _____

2. Ask at least three of your teammates:

- How confident are you in your game right now?

  _____

  _____

  _____

- From where do you get your confidence?

  _____

  _____

  _____

- What can I do or say as a captain to help you build your confidence when you have doubts?

  _____

  _____

  _____

COACH/CAPTAIN MEETING NOTES

_____

_____

_____

_____

_____

_____

_____

_____

_____

_____

_____

_____

_____

_____

_____

_____

_____

_____

_____

_____

_____

_____

_____

_____

_____

_____

_____

_____

_____

_____

_____

_____

_____

WEEK 7

Next Meeting Date:
Time:

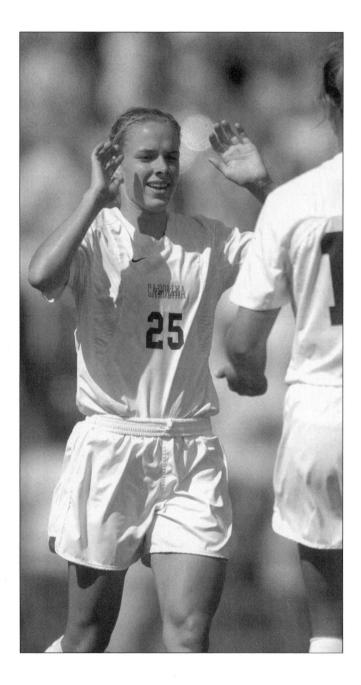

CHAPTER EIGHT

ENCOURAGER—REFOCUSER

HOW TO GET YOUR TEAMMATES BACK ON TRACK

*"Young players are leaders only when they are playing well . . .
that's not leadership. Anyone can lead the league in high fives when
things are going well. But during adversity, those times when things
are not going well, is when you need leaders in your group . . ."*
RICK PITINO, LOUISVILLE MEN'S BASKETBALL

WEEK
8

Real Leadership Is Leading Under Adversity

Your leadership skills will be tested and needed most when things aren't going well. It's easy to be a leader when you are winning, when your team chemistry is great, when everyone respects your coaches, and when you're playing well. It is a much different story when you're losing, your team can't get along, your teammates are frustrated with the coaches, and you're playing poorly. These are the times when you really must step up and make your presence felt as a Vocal Leader.

Remember how important your composure is during times of stress. When adversity strikes, your teammates and coaches will look to you to see your reaction and how you handle it. As Duke men's basketball coach Mike Krzyzewski says in his excellent book *Leading with the Heart*, "A leader has to show the face his team needs to see." You too must show your teammates you are calm, composed, and confident under pressure—the green light mindset we discussed earlier.

Once you take care of yourself, your next task is to take care of your teammates. In a perfect world, your teammates would be able to take care of themselves. However, many of them have a tendency to panic and self-destruct under pressure and adversity because they have not yet learned how to stay focused and mentally tough. Yes, it's not fair that you have to be responsible for keeping your teammates' heads in the game. But that is a big part of your job as a leader. You can't afford to get frustrated with them when they are already frustrated with themselves. If you let your frustration get the best of you, you will only make the situation more difficult for them. You have to be as patient as possible as you help them refocus their thinking on more positive and productive thoughts.

"Vocal leadership is so powerful. Remaining positive is the hardest part. It's easy to take on a negative tone. When I get frustrated, my tone changes and sometimes instead of encouraging people, it can break down. I am conscious of it, and I work at it because I am one of the more vocal players. It's my responsibility."
JULIE FOUDY, U.S. NATIONAL SOCCER TEAM

You will need to refocus the vast majority of your teammates when yellow and red light situations occur instead of letting them give up, choke, hide, or explode. You want to replace their pessimism with a sense of hope. In addition to hope, you also want to provide them with a simple and workable plan to help themselves get back on track. This chapter will provide you with a variety of proven strategies to help you refocus your teammates when they are frustrated, distracted, and discouraged.

Tune In to Your Teammates' Mindsets

A big key in helping your teammates refocus is to catch them as early as possible when they start to slip into the yellow light. Turning around yellow light situations is a lot less difficult than dealing with full blown red lights. As a Vocal Leader, you must be continually aware of your teammates' mindsets. Are they confident, focused, and positive or confused, frustrated, and passive? You must tune into the traffic light colors of each of your teammates. You have to be on the lookout for people who might be slipping into the yellow light. How can you tell?

Typically you can tell when your teammates are slipping into a yellow light by watching their body language. Their head will invariably be down and their shoulders will be hunched over. They will probably make very little eye contact with you and/or they will have a far-away or "deer in headlights" look in their eyes. This is because most athletes start focusing internally on their own thoughts and thinking too much when they are in a yellow.

Another way to tell when a teammate is in a yellow is by monitoring the pace at which they play. Most athletes have a certain rhythm and timing to their game when they are playing well. They do things at a regular pace. However, when athletes get into yellows and reds, most of them change their pace. The majority end up speeding up their pace—playing faster, taking more risks, and trying to force the issue. This faster pace only makes things worse because now they make mistakes at twice the speed. A few of your teammates might slow their pace and become much more passive and deliberate in their play. This too is a likely sign that they are not mentally where they need to be.

Tune In to Your Team's Momentum

You need to be aware of your individual teammates' mindsets as well as the momentum of the team overall. As a Vocal Leader, you want to be a catalyst to get your team on a positive roll and get the momentum going in your favor. You want to continually stoke the momentum with your compliments and ride the wave as long as you can. However, there will be times when the momentum is not going your way. These are the times when an opponent goes on an 8-0 run in basketball or volleyball, has a big five-run inning in baseball or softball, scores two quick goals in soccer or hockey, or has scored the last two touchdowns in football. It will be your job to sense the momentum turn, weather the storm, and step up and attempt to swing the momentum back in your favor.

Take Advantage of the Breaks in the Game

Use the natural breaks and down times during competition to check your teammates' mental traffic lights and to communicate with them. For example, the Duke men's basketball team does a great job of using free throw situations as an opportune time for a quick team huddle to keep everyone on track. Whether they are playing well or poorly, they always have a quick team huddle to reinforce what they are doing or to refocus. Similarly, volleyball teams can use the time between serves for a quick check-in and refocus the team if need be. Softball and baseball team leaders have ample time between pitches to keep the team focused. The main thing is to continually monitor the team's mindset and look to maintain or regain momentum.

WEEK 8

Stern or Sensitive?

Remember that each of your teammates will be different as to what approach works best for them. For a few teammates, you will need to get in their face and be more stern with them. "Get your head out of your %#@ and start playing," might be the only way to get through to some. For most, though, a much more sensitive approach will yield infinitely better results. Putting your arm around them and saying, "You're okay. Don't worry about it. Get the next one," will work for the majority of your teammates. Keep in mind the less confident your teammates are in themselves, the more sensitive and forgiving you need to be with them.

What you say and how you say it can make the difference between getting a teammate refocused on the game and getting them to focus their frustration on you. Use the information from the Teammate Mental Game Assessment you completed earlier to determine which approach will work best with each of your teammates.

With which teammates do I need to take a more stern approach?

_____

_____

_____

With which teammates do I need to take a more sensitive approach?

_____

_____

_____

"I think as a quarterback, you wear a lot of different hats, from motivator to leader, drill sergeant, encourager. Motivator is definitely one of them. And bringing that energy and enthusiasm to practice, getting those guys hungry, making sure they're finishing plays the right way and thinking about the right kind of things is part of my job. You can't motivate everyone the same way, everybody's got different triggers."

AARON RODGERS, GREEN BAY PACKERS

Six Strategies to Refocus Your Teammates

Once you sense your teammates are beginning to unravel, you need to step in and refocus them. Based on the same strategies you use to maintain your composure, here are six effective strategies you can use to get them back on track.

1. Control the Controllables

Most athletes get themselves into yellows and reds because they focus on variables they have very little control over—the uncontrollables. Here's a quick reminder of the uncontrollable factors that can distract, disrupt, and discourage your teammates.

> **UNCONTROLLABLES**—opponents, officials, crowd, coaches, teammates, parents, friends, playing time, injuries, illnesses, travel delays, scheduling, weather conditions, playing surface conditions, media, academic demands, seedings/rankings, etc.

Many athletes focus on these uncontrollable factors and get very frustrated. The problem is no matter how much energy and focus they devote to these factors, their energy is wasted because there is nothing they can do about them.

Instead, your job as a leader is to get your teammates to refocus on the variables they can do something about. Again, here is a reminder of some controllables.

CONTROLLABLES—effort, attitude, focus, confidence, commitment, communication, composure, diet, rest, preparation, reactions, stretching, etc.

For example, some teammates might be frustrated with your coach because of a lack of playing time. Your job is to help them recognize the controllables and uncontrollables in the situation. You might say something like, "I know you are frustrated with Coach Smith because you haven't been playing a lot lately. Instead of complaining about it to the rest of the team, I think you should go in and talk with him about it to find out exactly why you haven't been playing as much. I'm sure it would help, too, if you had a little better attitude about it in practices and did some of the extra work he has asked you to do."

Or you might be in a situation where an opponent is deliberately playing mind games with one of your teammates in an attempt to distract him from his game plan. You might say something like, "Larry, don't worry about him. Let your play do the talking. Stay composed and stick with your game plan. If you do that, you'll have the last laugh."

Remind your teammates to ignore, accept, and/or work around the factors that are outside of their control. You want to refocus them on the controllables because they are the only variables your teammates can realistically do anything about.

2. Focus on the Present

Another common reason why your teammates get into yellows and reds is because they dwell on their past mistakes. Many athletes dwell on past missed shots, poor passes, unforced errors, and previous mistakes and errors. Athletes who mentally get caught in the past cannot focus on the present plays. As a Vocal Leader, you have to help them let go of the past and refocus back on to the next play.

There are a variety of ways you can help your teammates get back to the present moment. Some simple phrases you can use include:

"Don't worry about it, get the next one."

"It only takes one."

"It's done. Battle this point."

"Right here, right now."

You can also use symbols to help them let go of the past. I often talk about mistakes as bricks that athletes carry around with them when they dwell on them. Instead of letting the brick weigh you down physically and mentally, you need to let it go and build something from the mistake. Fellow sport psych

WEEK 8

consultant Ken Ravizza talks about letting go of mistakes like flushing a toilet. You have to be able to clear out the crappy thinking and flush it away. You can remind your teammates to "Flush it!" Other athletes use symbols like taking a deep breath and blowing out the frustration of the past. Or you can physically touch your hand to your head as if you are hitting a mental reset button and getting your mind cleared of the past and focused on to the present. Whatever you choose to use, find something that your teammates can relate with and respond to.

Sometimes you will need to keep your team from focusing too much on a past win or championship. They might become complacent or too comfortable because they just won a big game or won a championship the previous season. When this is the case, some coaches have athletes put their awards from the previous season in a box so they feel like they need to prove something again for the next season.

While most athletes have problems dwelling on the past, some people focus too far ahead on the future and forget about the present moment. This often occurs when teams have a "big" competition coming up but a "minor" opponent they need to play before it. As a Vocal Leader, you must guard against complacency and overconfidence. You must refocus your team on the present game, not the one next weekend.

3. Focus on the Positive

Another mental mistake your teammates will make is to doubt themselves and expect negative things to happen. Your job as a leader is to plant positive seeds of success in their minds to replace the negative thoughts they might have.

For example, the Arizona Softball team was playing Oklahoma at the 2001 Women's College World Series in Oklahoma City. Down 4-0 in the sixth inning to defending national champion Oklahoma, Arizona senior third baseman Toni Mascarenas hit a three run home run, silencing the 7,000 plus Sooner fans in attendance.

After a solo shot by freshman Mackenzie Vandergeest to knot the score at 4-4 in the top of the seventh, Toni turned to shortstop Allison Andrade and told her, "You are going to make the game winning play. Don't worry about your hitting, Allie. I know you are going to make the game winning play." Allie had struck out twice and felt like she was letting the team down. However, Toni's words of encouragement picked her up and kept her positive and focused.

Arizona managed to push across another run in the top of the eighth to go ahead 5-4. However, Oklahoma loaded the bases in the bottom of the eighth. With two outs, the same swift Sooner second baseman who hit a home run in her previous at bat stepped into the batter's box. With the game on the line, she hit a ground ball between short and third. If the ball gets through the infield it's at least a tie game if not a win for Oklahoma. Third baseman Toni Mascarenas ranged to her left to make the play but the ball just got past her glove. Shortstop Allison Andrade ranged to her right and fielded the ball deep in the hole. She picked up the ball and, with her team's fate hanging in the balance, made a strong throw to first base which barely beat the runner by a mere fraction of a second. The Wildcats won the game in extra innings after coming back from a potentially disheartening 4-0 deficit and eventually won the national championship.

After the game, instead of taking the credit for hitting the key three run shot which put Arizona back into the game, Toni gushed over Allie for making the game winning play. "You did it Allie. You made the game winning play!" If it weren't for Toni's Vocal Leadership keeping Allie positive despite a tough day at the plate, who's to say what might have happened on that last play? Great leaders plant positive seeds of success in the minds of their teammates. They keep people positive and focused no matter how frustrating or bleak the situation might be.

4. Focus on the Process

By obsessing over outcomes, some of your teammates get into yellow and red lights because they put way too much pressure on themselves to perform. They feel pressure to perform for parents, friends, scouts, coaches, and teammates. Others will obsess over their stats and get caught up in the numbers and not in the game. The perfectionists on your team will feel like they have to make every play or they are letting everyone down. You will need to be able to deal with a variety of highly anxious and stressed out people. Your job is to keep things as simple and as manageable as possible for them. Remind them to take care of the process, and the outcomes they so desperately seek will take care of themselves.

As a Vocal Leader, get your team focused on executing three keys to the game as you head into each competition. These might be goals like outrebounding your opponents, making more free throws than your opponents attempt, and holding your opponents to less the 40% shooting in basketball. In baseball and softball you could use goals like getting ahead in the count for your pitchers, 100% fielding percentage, and having quality at bats as hitters.

Sometimes your entire team will get discouraged when you are down by a lot early in a competition. Instead of panicking, giving up, or trying to get it all back at once, refocus your teammates on slowly but surely chipping away at the lead. Remind them to stick with the game plan, play within themselves, and that you have plenty of time to get back into the game if you do it over time. Break down the seemingly impossible task of getting back in the game into manageable pieces you can accomplish over time. You want to give them a sense of hope and a workable plan.

WEEK 8

5. Playing with Perspective

Revisiting Chicken Little, some of your teammates will need a good dose of perspective when they think the sky is falling because they are in a slump, not getting playing time, or did not get a particular honor they felt they deserved. Although you are putting your heart and soul into it, you also must remind your teammates that it is just a game and that there are more important things in life.

Voted an all-conference player the previous year, Jenny found herself in a difficult slump. She tried everything to get out of it from extra practice, to adjusting her mechanics, to getting more sleep, to changing her lucky socks—but nothing worked. Each day she became more and more stressed about the situation which only made it worse. She worried that she was letting down everyone including her teammates, coaches, parents, and friends. Seeing that she was definitely frustrated, Amy, the captain of the team, invited Jenny to come with her before practice. "Where are we going?" asked Jenny. "You'll see," said Amy.

Amy drove Jenny a few miles off campus to the local hospital. They went inside and up to the 4th floor. As the elevator doors opened, Jenny saw a sign that said "Children's Cancer Wing." Amy took Jenny around to the various rooms to sign autographs and to talk with the kids and their families. Despite some of the children being very ill, their faces lit up when Amy and Jenny entered the room. After about 45 minutes, Amy and Jenny said their goodbyes to the kids and headed back to campus for practice. As they got into the car, Amy turned to Jenny and said, "So, what do you think?" With tears in her eyes Jenny said, "I can't believe how selfish I was worrying about my slump when these kids are dealing with something so much worse than I am. Thanks for showing me how good I really have it."

Jenny started playing again with a whole new sense of perspective. As you might guess, with her renewed mindset she focused on enjoying the game and having fun again and quickly got out of her slump. Without saying much, Amy taught Jenny an important lesson in sport and life.

6. Focus on the Message, Not the Messenger

Some of your teammates are likely going to get in yellows and reds when they are receiving criticism from your coaches. They will feel frustrated that the coach is unnecessarily picking on them. Or they will be discouraged by the negative feedback because their confidence in themselves is being shaken. Help them understand that your coach must believe in them enough because he/she is providing them with feedback. Help them filter the criticism so they can focus on the message conveyed rather than taking it personally.

7. Take the Problem Off Them and Put it on Yourself

Finally, when mistakes and problems occur, step up and take the responsibility for them rather than pointing the finger at your teammates. Many times the situation won't be your fault. But by taking the blame and responsibility for the problem, you can then get your teammates to mentally move on and concentrate on more important things, rather than worrying about who to blame.

Chapter Eight Summary

Being a Refocuser for your team is a difficult and time-consuming job. But it's one that you will need to execute often because there are always challenges, obstacles, and adversities which can lead your teammates astray. Stay mentally tough yourself and refocus them back on the task at hand.

KEY POINTS FROM CHAPTER EIGHT

List three to five major points or insights you gained from this chapter:

1. _____

2. _____

3. _____

4. _____

5. _____

PRACTICAL EXERCISES FOR CHAPTER EIGHT

1. Interview a captain from another team. Ask them:

• What situations typically frustrate and distract your teammates?

_____

_____

_____

• What do you try to do or say as a captain to keep people on track?

_____

_____

_____

WEEK
8

2. Make a list of the typical situations when your team tends to get frustrated, distracted, and out of sync: (poor calls from officials, road games, poor weather, adverse playing conditions, unsportsmanlike opponents, slow start, etc.) Then write down a specific plan of what you can do or say to refocus the team when these situations arise. Review this plan with your coach.

1. Challenging Situation _____

_____

Refocusing Plan_____

_____

_____

2. Challenging Situation _____

_____

Refocusing Plan_____

_____

_____

3. Challenging Situation _____

_____

Refocusing Plan_____

_____

_____

4. Challenging Situation _____

_____

Refocusing Plan_____

_____

_____

5. Challenging Situation _____

_____

Refocusing Plan_____

_____

COMPANION ONLINE LEADERSHIP RESOURCE

**For more information,
visit www.TeamCaptainsNetwork.com**

COACH/CAPTAIN MEETING NOTES

WEEK 8

Next Meeting Date:
Time:

CHAPTER NINE

ENCOURAGER—TEAM BUILDER

HOW TO BUILD A WINNING TEAM CHEMISTRY

"If you want to build an atmosphere in which everybody pulls together to win, then you, as a leader have to recognize that it all starts with you. It starts with your attitude, your commitment, your caring, your passion for excellence, your dedication to winning. It starts with the example you set."
PAT WILLIAMS, SENIOR EXECUTIVE VICE PRESIDENT, ORLANDO MAGIC

The fourth and final aspect of being an Encourager for your team is to promote and encourage great team chemistry. As a Vocal Leader, it is up to you to create an environment in which your teammates respect and trust each other. Of course, not everyone is always going to get along with each other or want to hang out together. That's both natural and okay. You do, though, want to create an environment in which people feel a sense of family and belonging to something special. Here are some ideas that will help you create a sense of unity and chemistry on your team.

WEEK 9

How to Get Your Team to Commit to a Common Goal

1. Establish a Common Goal

Before your season starts, invest the time to establish a common goal with your teammates and with the help of your coach. Find out what they really want to achieve for your upcoming season. By involving your teammates in determining your goals for the season, you are much more likely to get their commitment to your team's goals. They will be motivated to pursue them because they value them and had a say in creating them.

To determine a common goal with your teammates, break up your team into three groups with an equal representation of the veterans and newcomers in each group. Have each of the three groups come up with a response to the following questions: "What could we achieve if we really put things together this season?" Or, "What's possible if we play up to our potential this season?" Give each of the groups roughly 10–15 minutes to discuss and debate their answers. Then have each of the groups share their goals and the reasons why they think they are possible. After each of the three groups have given their responses, look for similarities between the three groups and see if you can come to a consensus as a team over your season's goals. Typically, all three groups will be in the same ballpark in regard to your team's goals. These could include goals like winning a conference/state/national championship, winning all of your home games, placing in the top three of your conference/state/nationals, having a grade point average of 3.0 or above, winning half of your conference matches, etc.

The key is to set team goals that are both realistic and challenging based on where your program is in terms of its development. If your program has a winning tradition and you made it to Regionals last year, perhaps your goal is to advance further and make it to Nationals. Or if your program is in a rebuilding phase, perhaps you want to focus on placing in the top half of your conference. Having three different groups share their opinions typically helps to ensure that your goals are both realistic and challenging.

2. Clarify the Commitments and Standards You Need to Get There

Once you have established a clear and compelling goal to pursue for the season, you then need to discuss the commitments and standards it will take to get there. You must both establish where you want to go and how you will get there. This is one of the most important yet most neglected aspects of goal setting. You need to clarify the commitments you will make to each other to best position your team to achieve the goals you set.

Again, ask this question to your three different groups: "What are the 10 most important commitments we will need to make to each other throughout the season to give us the best chance of reaching our goal?" The three groups will again discuss and debate the 10 most important commitments that will help your team achieve the goal. Have each group share their thoughts as you look to come to a consensus agreement on the 10 or so commitments.

(Ten is not a rigid number. You can go with as little as eight or as many as 12. You need enough to make a difference but not too many where they start to lose emphasis.)

Your teammates will likely mention commitments like—we need to:

- consistently give our best effort in sport and school

- respect our teammates and coaches and handle conflict constructively

- take care of our bodies and stay away from alcohol and other drugs

- listen to and trust our coaches

- understand and accept our roles and play them to the best of our ability

3. Create a Mission Statement and Commitment Contract

Finally, after you have invested the time to determine where you want to go with your season and what kind of commitments it will take to get there, list all of the information on a sheet of paper. Hand it out to each of your teammates so they are very clear about your goals and your commitments. If any of them have any concerns over what is listed, they need to speak up now to address the concerns. If no one has any concerns, then you should have everyone's "buy in" to your goals and commitments.

To signify everyone's commitment, have your teammates come up one by one to sign the Commitment Contract. Remind them their signature signifies they are making a solemn commitment to themselves, their teammates, and the coaches, to passionately pursue these goals and abide by and hold their teammates accountable to the commitments listed. The Commitment Contract should signify that everyone is both literally and figuratively on the same page. (See the example on the next page.)

Once everyone has signed the document, you can frame and hang it in a spot in your locker room where your teammates will see it often. Some teams even like to put everyone's picture around the paper to give it more of a personal touch. You can also shrink the contract down to wallet-size, laminate it or put it in a luggage tag, and give everyone a copy to put on their bag or to keep it with them as a continual reminder. The Commitment Contract must become a document you live every day, not something you do at the beginning of the season then throw in a drawer never to be seen again.

WEEK 9

In addition to getting clarity and commitment to your team's goals, as a leader you also get another benefit when you create a Commitment Contract. By making this public commitment and signing their names to it, you will have a much easier time holding your teammates accountable to do what they said and signed they would do. The Commitment Contract gives you some good hard evidence to use if and when your teammates decide to bend or break any of the listed commitments. We'll talk more about this in the upcoming Enforcer section.

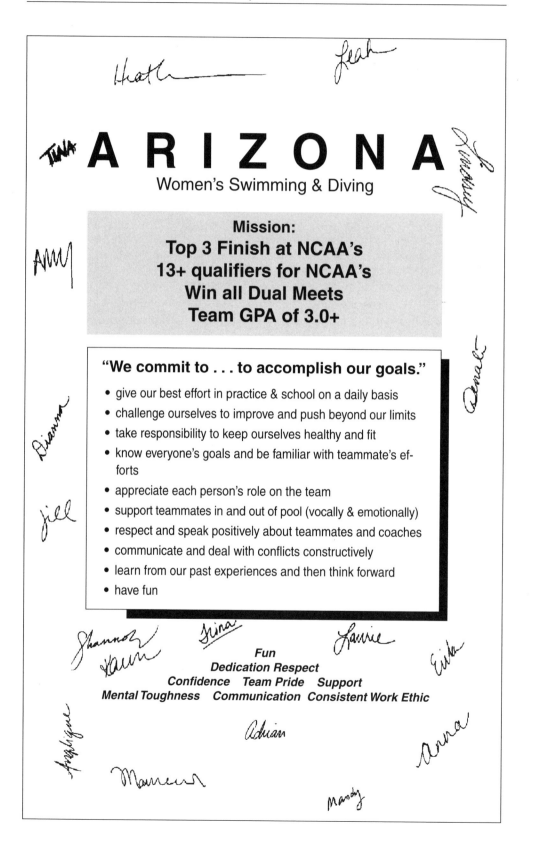

ARIZONA
Women's Swimming & Diving

Mission:
Top 3 Finish at NCAA's
13+ qualifiers for NCAA's
Win all Dual Meets
Team GPA of 3.0+

"We commit to . . . to accomplish our goals."

- give our best effort in practice & school on a daily basis
- challenge ourselves to improve and push beyond our limits
- take responsibility to keep ourselves healthy and fit
- know everyone's goals and be familiar with teammate's efforts
- appreciate each person's role on the team
- support teammates in and out of pool (vocally & emotionally)
- respect and speak positively about teammates and coaches
- communicate and deal with conflicts constructively
- learn from our past experiences and then think forward
- have fun

Fun
Dedication Respect
Confidence   Team Pride   Support
Mental Toughness   Communication   Consistent Work Ethic

Post the team Commitment Contract in a very prominent spot so your teammates will see it daily. The contract will serve as a continual reminder about where your team wants to go, what it will take to get there, and that everyone is committed to doing their part. Throughout the season, it is your job to continually remind and refocus the team on living up to the commitments it will take to reach your team's goals.

How to Help Your Teammates Accept Their Roles

Another responsibility you have as a Team Builder is to help your teammates accept their roles. It is easy for the starters to accept their roles because they are getting exactly what they want—playing time. It's a lot tougher for the players on your team who get limited, inconsistent, or nonexistent playing time to accept their roles.

"Sometimes the player's greatest challenge is coming to grips with his role on the team."

Scottie Pippen, Chicago Bulls

Getting people to accept their roles depends on two factors: 1. Clearly defining their role, 2. Showing appreciation for their role. Your coach will take care of the first part as good coaches invest the time to communicate and clarify each person's role on the team. This is usually done a month or so into the season when the preseason is drawing to a close. Typically by that time your coach has seen what people can do and he/she will begin to settle on a regular lineup.

The appreciation part is where Vocal Leaders come in. Your job is to help the people who don't get to play as much feel they are still an important part of the team. You need to vocally acknowledge and appreciate all of the big and little things they do for the team. They need this praise and attention more than your starters do because it is easy for the reserves to feel underappreciated and neglected. Call attention to the effort they give in practice and especially the effort they might give supporting your teammates from the sidelines. Let them know how much you appreciate their words of encouragement and advice during huddles. And, if you get media interviews, look to mention the people who don't always get a lot of attention or credit. It will mean a lot to them.

WEEK 9

"I long ago learned that publicly acknowledging the people who don't get a lot of the limelight does wonders for team morale. You must make these people know you not only are aware of their efforts, you appreciate them."

Rick Pitino, Louisville Men's Basketball

Show Appreciation with Awards

You might even want to create some awards that are designed to appreciate the many roles that need to be played to help a team be successful. These awards should not be based on playing time and can be voted on by the team. Some categories you might consider using are:

- **Practice Player of the Week**—this award goes to the person who was the best performer in practice during the week, regardless of playing time in the games.

- **Nails Award**—this award goes to the player who was mentally tough as nails. This might go to a teammate who has been sitting out, but worked really hard through some grueling rehab and stayed focused on getting herself back and ready to play as soon as possible.

- **Glue Award**—this award goes to the person who did a great job of putting the team first and was the glue that bound the team together. Again, this could go to a person who was very involved in the game even though they were sitting on the bench. Or it might go to a person who took the servant leader philosophy and did a lot for their teammates.

You can create whatever award you see fit that will bring attention to the roles and individuals vital to your team's success—but who don't always get the proper attention they deserve.

Team Bonding

Finally, as a Vocal Leader, look to set up opportunities where your teammates can hang out and get to know each other better outside of practice time. Team bonding is especially important if you have a number of subgroups within your team. As a Vocal Leader, it is your job to build bridges between the various subgroups on your team: veterans and newcomers, people of different socioeconomic backgrounds, and people of different races, ethnicities, and religions. You want to help these various teammates understand they have a lot more in common than what is different. Instead of these subgroups splintering off and becoming cliques within the team, you want to pull each of the subgroups together so everyone understands you are one team focused on a common goal.

"A sure thing to break down a team is little cliques. It's easy to have the younger players in one group and the older players in another group. On any trip we go on, the veterans make a point of just sitting with the younger players and talking with them. It would be so easy to stay in our comfort zone and hang out with the people we've been playing with for ten years. So we sit with the younger players at lunch and talk with them. It's easy after you have broken the ice."

Julie Foudy, U.S. Soccer National Team

Team Building Activities and Ideas

There are a wide variety of activities you can organize to help your teammates build a better bond. You can organize simple social events like going to the movies, bowling, watching a favorite TV show together, or more adventurous activities like white water rafting, paint ball, laser tag, ropes course, etc. These activities are fun and give your teammates a chance to see different sides of each other they might not normally see during practices. So be sure not to exclude anyone when you plan these events.

Team Retreat

You can plan a preseason team retreat as a fun way to kick off your season. Go to a local park for a day or reserve a cabin or campsite in the woods for an overnight event. Pick a date and time that everyone can attend and make it a fun yet meaningful event for everyone. Plan a mixture of fun and adventurous activities along with some time for discussion and reflection. You can look to establish your goals for the season and draft a Commitment Contract. You can also have people share some of their most memorable moments, most embarrassing moments, and/or the people who have had the biggest impact on their lives. Give people an opportunity to get to know each other at a deeper level. A good team retreat can go a long way in setting a positive and productive tone for your season.

Team Dinner

You can also arrange occasional team dinners. A good idea is to do it potluck style where everyone is responsible for bringing a specific dish/beverage. You'll have fun plus it also sends the message that if everyone contributes something, the entire team will ultimately benefit.

Family Pictures

You can ask each of your teammates to bring in a picture of their family. Go around the room and give each person roughly five minutes or so to introduce their family—talking about their interests, occupations, ages, etc. Encourage each teammate to briefly describe their relationship with each family member and tell who they think they are the most like and why. You will discover a lot about your teammates. At times this exercise can get quite emotional as people talk about their families.

WEEK 9

Support Squad

A practical and easy way to help your teammates get to know each other better throughout the season is to set up a Support Squad. Simply pair up each of your teammates with another person on the team. Rotate the pairings each week so that everyone will spend at least one week with every person on the team.

At the beginning of the week, invest five minutes to have the pairs meet to answer and discuss three sections:

1. Challenge me to . . .

In this section, partners should look to create a measurable challenge they would like their partner to hold them accountable to achieving for the week. For example, one player may want to successfully complete nine out of 10 repetitions of a specific drill. The other partner may want to focus on completing 100% of the weight workouts with quality—without skipping or being sloppy on a single rep. This gives each person a specific goal for the week as well as a partner to assist them and hold them accountable.

2. Support me if I struggle with . . .

Partners should tell each other about possible things that could distract, discourage, or frustrate them during the week. For example, one of the players might have a big test on Thursday. They are worried about doing well on it because it is a big part of their grade and they didn't do well on the first test. Hopefully their partner would offer to help them study for it. The other person might be struggling with a nagging injury that hasn't healed fully. Their partner could remind them to rehab, get taped, and stretch properly while warming up. The benefit is that both partners clue in each other to potential distractions and ask for their teammate's help and support.

3. If I get frustrated/discouraged, remind me to . . .

Finally, should their partner see them getting in a yellow or red light, they also need to let the person know the best way to approach them to help them get back on track. They tell their partner if they should be stern or sensitive. The also let them know specific words, phrases, or gestures to use to help the person refocus and get back into a green light. As you can see, this part is especially beneficial for Vocal Leaders because you will learn exactly what to do or say for each teammate as you get paired up with them during the course of the season.

(Author's Note: These are just a few of the numerous ideas you can do to build a unified and cohesive team. If you are looking for additional ideas and activities to promote team chemistry, check with your coach to see if he/she already has my books *Championship Team Building* and *Jeff Janssen's Peak Performance Playbook*. Both of these resources contain dozens of fun and interactive ideas to assist you with your team building efforts. If not, you can order by visiting www.janssensportsleadership.com or calling 1-888-721-TEAM.)

COMPANION ONLINE LEADERSHIP RESOURCE

For more information,
visit www.TeamCaptainsNetwork.com

Chapter Nine Summary

Team building is yet another responsibility you have as a Vocal Leader. Establish and build your teammates' commitment around a common goal, help them understand and accept their roles, and give them an opportunity to bond with each other. Remember, it takes a team to reach a dream.

KEY POINTS FROM CHAPTER NINE

List three to five major points or insights you gained from this chapter:

1. _____

2. _____

3. _____

4. _____

5. _____

PRACTICAL EXERCISES FOR CHAPTER NINE

1. Organize a team building event for your team over the next week. You can host a team dinner, have people over to watch a movie, lead an experiential team building exercise before or after practice, go bowling, etc. Do something fun that brings your team together.

2. Find a coach whose teams always seem to have great team chemistry. Ask the coach:

• Is team chemistry important to you? Why?

_____

_____

_____

• What are some problems that get in the way of good team chemistry?

_____

_____

_____

WEEK 9

- What do you do to build and maintain team chemistry?

_____

_____

_____

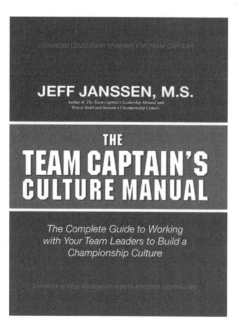

For more information on how to build better team chemistry and a Championship Culture in your program, check out our advanced Team Captain's Culture Manual at www.janssensportsleadership.com/resources/team-captains-culture-manual/

COACH/CAPTAIN MEETING NOTES

_____

_____

_____

_____

_____

_____

_____

_____

_____

_____

_____

_____

_____

_____

_____

_____

_____

_____

_____

_____

_____

_____

_____

_____

_____

_____

**WEEK
9**

Next Meeting Date:
Time:

CHAPTER TEN

ENFORCER

HOW TO MINIMIZE AND MANAGE TEAM CONFLICT

"The entire aim of our policies at Tennessee is to get our players to discipline each other. . . . We have evolved a system in which . . . I don't have to do a whole lot of punishing, penalizing, or pushing them. Our upperclassmen become the disciplinarians of our team instead of me."
PAT SUMMITT, FORMER TENNESSEE WOMEN'S BASKETBALL COACH

Respected Vocal Leaders not only need to establish the team's commitments and rules, they also need to enforce them. This means you must hold yourself and your teammates accountable to follow your team's rules and standards. You must be willing to stand up and speak out when your teammates aren't living up to their responsibilities. You must insist they walk their talk. Constructively confronting teammates is an often uncomfortable and unpleasant role Vocal Leaders must play, but one that is absolutely critical to your team's chemistry, commitment, and success. This section provides you with several effective strategies to help you and your teammates effectively deal with conflict.

WEEK 10

Conflict Is Inevitable: Deal with It

Keep in mind conflict is an inevitable part of being on a team. Whenever you get a variety of people together with different backgrounds, attitudes, and opinions who are competing with and against each other for playing time and respect over the long course of a sometimes turbulent season, you can't help but have conflict. Expect all kinds of conflict to flare up throughout your season between a variety of groups and individuals: athletes and coaches, athletes and athletes, coaches and coaches, parents and athletes, parents and coaches, etc. You will never be able to avoid some kind of conflict within a team. It's impossible.

Certainly each team and season are different. However, almost every team experiences the same basic conflicts. The three most likely conflict situations you will have to deal with as a captain include:

1. Confronting teammates who are not working as hard as they should be in practices, the weight room, conditioning, rehab, the classroom, etc.

2. Confronting teammates who break team policies: drinking, curfew, skipping classes, missing workouts, etc.

3. Confronting teammates who are in conflict with coaches and other athletes: disagreements over playing time, feeling like a coach is picking on them, problems with roommates, jealousies, communication problems, etc.

I can virtually guarantee you these conflicts will occur at least once if not several times throughout the course of your season. If you are going to be an effective Vocal Leader, you must get comfortable dealing with these uncomfortable situations. This chapter provides you with several strategies to help you deal with these common conflicts plus any others which might arise.

Keep "The Main Thing" the Main Thing

The key to dealing with conflict is learning how to handle it constructively. This means finding ways to discuss it, deal with it, and move on. Successful teams have conflict. They just are able to keep their primary focus on their common goal as they work through the conflict. Whatever happens, the players understand the common goal always takes precedence and the conflict becomes secondary. Unsuccessful teams do the exact opposite. They make the conflict the priority and let the drama distract them from their common goal. Your job as a leader is to continually remind and refocus your teammates (and coaches) back on your common goal as you work through the conflict.

"Happiness is not the absence of conflict but the ability to deal with it effectively."

ANONYMOUS

Don't Sacrifice Being Respected for Being Liked

Many people cringe at the hint of conflict. They try to avoid or ignore it, hoping it will somehow magically take care of itself. Sometimes it subsides on its own but most of the time it only gets worse if you choose to ignore it. Most people avoid conflict because they don't want to hurt other people's feelings. More often, it is because people are afraid that others will not like them. As we discussed in the beginning, as a leader you must have the confidence and self-assurance to not be overly concerned about what others think. As a leader, it will be impossible to please everyone all of the time. Your job is not to make everyone happy. Your job is to do the right thing, encourage others to do the right thing, and confront those who don't. Focus more on gaining your teammates' respect than trying to have them like you all of the time. Don't sacrifice your principles for popularity.

"You're never going to be the most popular guy on the team—especially since part of your job will be to deliver the occasional unpleasant message—so don't even bother to try. It's respect you need, not popularity."
JOE MONTANA, LEGENDARY NFL QUARTERBACK

Having the Courage to Confront

In essence, when you have the courage to constructively confront your teammates, you show them you care enough about the team's success and well-being that you are willing to overcome your uncomfortable feelings regarding conflict. Because you want what is best for the team and you have invested so much of yourself into it, you are willing to tackle the tough issues so they can be dealt with and resolved. Discipline isn't something you do to someone—it's something you do for their own good and the good of the team.

If you don't address various conflict situations because of your fear or uncomfortable feelings, you are basically saying your comfort level in not addressing the conflict is more important than the team's success and well-being. That's selfish and not the mark of a true leader. Further, if you don't address the problems, your teammates who are doing the right thing will likely lose their respect for you because you aren't willing to stand up for what's right. And, if you are so concerned about having people like you, wouldn't you rather have the people who are doing the right thing like you than those few who aren't?

"Confrontation is good. It simply means meeting the truth head-on."
MIKE KRZYZEWSKI, DUKE MEN'S BASKETBALL

WEEK
10

More Encouraging Leads to Less Enforcing

Interestingly, what you find with conflict is that the more you play the role of Encourager with your teammates when they do the right thing, the less you will have to be an Enforcer. They will want to do the right thing because they want to earn and maintain your praise and respect. If you Encourage 75% of the time, you will likely need to Enforce only 25% of the time, if not less.

Here's a graduated approach to encouraging and enforcing your team's rules and standards with your teammates. You'll notice a more serious and harsh tone is necessary as you advance through the steps.

1. Start by Encouraging

Encouraging your teammates will be enough to keep the majority of them in line. You might say something like, "I loved your effort today in practice. You worked hard from start to finish and challenged yourself and your teammates on every drill. That's going to pay off for you individually and for our team—great job!" Most of your teammates (roughly 60%) will respond well to your encouragement and it will motivate them to continue working hard.

2. Move to Reminding and Refocusing

Those who aren't responding to the regular encouragement might need a little reminder and some refocusing. You might say something like, "Hey team, this has been a pretty sloppy practice thus far. Let's pick it up right now and get our heads back in the game." Or, "Matt, you are a lot better player than what you are showing. It's time to stop feeling sorry for yourself and start playing like you know how." Hopefully this will let your teammates know they have fallen below what is expected of them and they need to refocus themselves to get back on track. Communicating to your teammates in this way should get another segment (another 20% or so) of your team back in line.

"There are a lot of ways to deliver a message without being overly confrontational. Even when you're getting on somebody, you can do it in a way that will build him up. 'Come on, you're better than that.' 'How can you let a guy like that beat you? He can't carry your helmet.' Stuff like that. You're showing respect for him at the same time you're delivering a message."
JOE MONTANA, LEGENDARY NFL QUARTERBACK

In his book, *Heads Up Baseball*, sport psych consultant Ken Ravizza encourages athletes to use the Two Minute Drill to get refocused. When you sense your team is losing its focus and playing sloppy, catch them during a water break or bring them in for a quick huddle. Challenge them to refocus themselves and put things back together again for the next two minutes. This challenge brings them back to the present moment and gives them a manageable goal to focus on over the next two minutes. In most cases your teammates will be able to change around the momentum of the practice and get back on track. Build off of the success for two minutes and challenge them to continue staying focused throughout the rest of the practice in two minute segments at a time.

3. Drawing the Line—This Is Unacceptable

If some people still aren't responding, you might need to go to a third level of enforcement. This is where you draw the line and let people know very clearly that what they are doing is a problem. Take them aside and say something like, "This is unacceptable. You made a commitment to this team to give your best effort and you are not getting it done. Get your act together now. It's time to go hard or go home." This phrasing should leave no doubt as to what needs to happen. By this time, at least 90% if not 100% of your team should be back on track.

4. Involve Your Coach

Finally, if a person still refuses to honor your requests and reprimands, you often have no choice but to make your coach aware of the situation. Odds are, your coach is already aware of the situation and the problems the person is causing. Just about every team tends to have one or two high-maintenance, resistant individuals (the final 10%) who are difficult for captains and coaches to handle.

Inform your coach of the steps you have taken. Then it is up to your coach to use his/her authority to hold the person accountable. This could include consequences like talking with the person, not starting them or withholding playing time, suspending them from practices/games, to dismissal from the team. You have to trust that your coach will seriously address the person and the problem. Your coach will want to see your respect as a leader bolstered, not undermined.

The Five Conflict Styles

As a Vocal Leader, you have a variety of options at your disposal for how to manage a conflict situation, ranging from ignoring the problem to all out confrontation. Understand that you have a choice in how you want to approach potential conflict situations. The choice you make dictates your chances of resolving the issue. There is no particular ideal way to handle conflict. The best way to proceed depends on the unique factors of the particular situation. The key involves choosing the "best" way to handle the situation considering both short and long term consequences.

To help leaders better understand their various choices when faced with conflict, I like to use a model described by Dr. David Johnson in his book, *Reaching Out*. The model shows five different styles you can use when approaching a conflict situation. Your approach to conflict depends on your answers to two critical questions:

1. How important is it that I get what I want?

2. How important is my relationship with the other person?

Almost all conflict between people can be boiled down to these two simple questions. "How badly do I want my needs and goals met?" And, "How important is it that I maintain a friendly relationship with this other person?"

WEEK
10

Let's take a look at each of the styles. Johnson uses animal analogies that accurately depict the different styles of conflict resolution. I think you'll find the animal analogies both humorous and helpful in understanding the various approaches.

Avoiding (Turtle)

Turtles seek to avoid conflict at all costs. They crawl into their shells, thereby ignoring and avoiding conflict. By doing so, they hope conflict will eventually subside or go away on its own. Turtles rate both their goals and the relationship as having low importance. Avoiding conflict situations can be a good style to use when faced with minor, insignificant issues. However, most of the time the conflict never gets resolved.

Smoothing (Teddy Bear)

Teddy Bears want to maintain a good relationship with the other person when faced with conflict and are willing to give up their personal goals to do so. They often give in to teammates in order to maintain a friendly relationship. They seek to minimize conflict by giving up what they want. These are the athletes who tend to get walked on and used by their more aggressive teammates. However, these are also the athletes who do a good job of keeping the team together during disagreements. Smoothing is a good style to use when the issue is of minor importance while the relationship is of utmost importance.

Competing (Shark)

Sharks seek to get their own way in conflict situations, often at the expense of the other person. Their main priority is to achieve their goals and they do not worry if they step on someone and hurt their feelings to get what they want. While you can admire the aggressiveness and tenacity of sharks, they often leave a bloody trail of offended and upset teammates in their wake. Competing is a great style to use when playing against other teams but it can have problematic consequences within your team. While the shark approach is best kept to a minimum on the team, occasionally you might need to harshly confront a teammate when someone does something that is totally out of line.

Compromising (Fox)

Foxes are willing to give up some of their goals in order to maintain a friendly relationship. They are open to negotiating and are focused on finding a fair agreement for both parties. Foxes are often a good thing to have on a team with various wants. Because they are willing to compromise, they will eat at your favorite restaurant today if you agree to eat at their favorite restaurant tomorrow.

Collaborating (Owl)

The wise old owls are focused on helping the other person get what they want as well as meeting their own needs. They take the time to find solutions that fully and mutually satisfy both people. Owls are often a rare bird on teams but certainly a prized possession.

Which Style Is Best?

Remember, no one style is best. The particular style you choose depends on the situation. Sometimes it may be appropriate to be a shark while other situations may call for being a turtle. Additionally, while you will use one or two of the styles more often than the others, you will probably need to use all five styles at various points throughout your season.

Which style do you tend to use when you are in a conflict with your parents?

_____

_____

Which style do you tend to use when you are in a conflict with your friends?

_____

_____

Which style do you tend to use when you are in a conflict with your coach?

_____

_____

Which style do you tend to use when you are in a conflict with your teammates?

_____

_____

The best way to decide which style to use is to go back to the two original questions:

1. How important is it that I get what I want?

2. How important is my relationship with the other person?

As you might have guessed, the most successful leaders are focused on meeting their goals AND are sensitive to their relationships with their teammates. Thus, you should look to compromise and collaborate as much as possible. Save the shark for more serious situations after you have first Encouraged.

WEEK 10

Six Steps for Resolving Conflict

Here is an overall framework for you to use when you are trying to resolve a conflict on your team.

1. Define the problem.

Be sure that you have clearly defined the problem or conflict. Conflicts within teams start superficially but are often just the symptoms of deeper problems involving a lack of respect, trust, and appreciation.

2. Brainstorm possible solutions.

Collectively come up with several potential solutions. Try to see the problem from a variety of viewpoints. Reserve your judgment on the ideas until several have been generated.

3. Evaluate possible solutions.

Look over the possible solutions and determine the expected consequences of each.

4. Decide on a solution.

Collectively try to agree on the best way to handle the conflict.

5. Implement the solution.

Put the solution into action.

6. Evaluate the success of the solution.

Monitor and critique the success of the agreed upon solution. If it works, you have successfully resolved your conflict. If it did not work out, you need to return to steps one, two, or three.

Picking Your Battles

Tolerance is a key component of any successful team. You and your teammates need to respect and put up with the many different personalities which make up the team. Some teammates will be outgoing, outspoken, zany, and talkative. Others will be more quiet, shy, and solitary. It's important to understand that people have a lot of different preferences and quirks which make them unique. Teammates must appreciate each other's differences and learn to value people for who they are. Team tolerance should occur in a variety of different areas including music preferences, clothing styles, sleeping habits, and anything that has little direct effect on the team reaching its goal.

Deciding when to be tolerant and when to confront can be difficult. The key to making the correct decision can often be discovered by asking yourself the following question, "Are the person's decisions or actions interfering with the team's success or chemistry in a significant manner?"

You must address certain issues that can get in the way of your team's success, chemistry, and well-being. These include problems like being late for practice, slacking off in conditioning, missing rehab appointments, not going to classes, getting poor grades, wasting time at study tables, talking about teammates and coaches behind their backs, using and/or abusing alcohol and other drugs, being promiscuous and giving the team a bad reputation, cheating on tests, etc. If you don't address these issues in a firm, fair, and consistent manner, your team's standards will continually be lowered until eventually your teammates will be able to get away with anything. It is much better to deal with these problems as early as possible and nip them in the bud—before they mushroom into much bigger problems. The next section provides you with some suggestions for constructive confrontation.

Ten Tips for Constructive Conflict

Here are ten tips to keep in mind when you are about to approach a teammate with a potential conflict.

1. Begin with agreement.

When you are in a conflict with someone, try to find some areas where you do agree to start off on a friendly note. Then begin to explore and discuss areas where you disagree.

2. Confront in the spirit to help.

Your primary reason for confronting a person should be to show them how their actions are adversely affecting you and/or the team. Confront in an effort to improve or alleviate problems.

3. Check it out before accusing.

Check with the person to see if your information is correct before accusing them. "Jim, I heard from a reliable source that you were out until 2:00 a.m. the night before our game. Is this true?"

4. See it from their side.

When confronting someone, try to see the situation from their perspective first. You don't always have to agree with their viewpoint, but start with the effort to truly understand it.

5. Attack the problem, not the person.

When you confront, be sure you are focused on dealing with the problem, not hurling personal insults and trying to put the other person in their place.

WEEK 10

6. Handle conflicts individually in private.

It is often best to handle your personal disagreements in a private setting, not in a public forum. This way you will not have the pressure of other people listening in and making the situation more complex.

7. Keep control of yourself and your emotions.

Sometimes it is better to wait to address conflicts. The heat of the moment and high emotions can cause people to say and do things they might regret later. Avoid dealing with conflict right after a game. It is often best to wait until the next day. Take some time to cool down and approach the situation with a level head.

8. Don't discuss the problem with everyone else.

This is often a big problem in team settings. It is much easier to complain about a person to others than it is to confront the person. Constructively discuss the situation with the person you are having a conflict with rather than infecting and dividing the rest of the team.

9. Stick to the point.

Keep your discussion focused on the single issue at hand. Too many times people dredge up past irrelevant disagreements. Bringing up past problems complicates the original issue and often escalates the conflict.

10. Sometimes you have to agree to disagree.

Despite your best efforts, not all conflicts will be able to be resolved. At times you will just have to agree to disagree and move on.

How to Use the "DESC" Formula to Control Conflict

DESC is a simple formula that can help you control conflict (Greenberg, 1990). The formula is designed to help you get your goals and needs across in an assertive way while also respecting and maintaining a good relationship with the other person. It is a great way to help turtles address conflict, teddy bears assert their needs more forcefully, and sharks be more sensitive and tactful. Try this formula the next time you are faced with a conflict situation.

D = Describe the situation.

Describe the concern/problem/behavior objectively and accurately to the other person.

You can start this by using the word "When . . . " Example—"When you are not running and working as hard as you could be during conditioning . . . "

E = Express your feelings.

Express to the other person how the situation makes you feel.

Use "I feel . . . " Example—"I feel frustrated, angry, and cheated . . . "

S = Specify what you would like to happen.

Tell the other person what you would prefer.

Use the words "I would like/prefer . . . " Example—"I would like it if you would pick it up and run the way you are capable of . . . "

C = Consequences.

Tell the person the expected consequences if they do what was specified.

Use the words, "If you do . . . " Example—"If you do, I think we will be able to outlast teams at the end of games which gives us a better shot of winning the conference championship we are working toward."

Additionally, you may want to begin by using the person's name and demonstrate some understanding and empathy to their situation to help them be more open to your message.

Putting it all together:

"John, I realize finals are coming up and you have been up late studying at the library. However, when you are not running or working hard during conditioning, I feel frustrated and angry because it seems as if you are cheating our team. I would like you to pick it up and run the way you are capable of. If you do, I think we have a much better chance of outlasting teams at the end of games which gives us a better shot of winning the conference championship that we are working toward."

DESC is designed to clearly get your message across while still being sensitive and tactful as you demonstrate respect for the other person. Of course, you will not handle every situation this way, but it does provide you with a good framework to use when you want to assertively and tactfully get your message across.

Mediator with Teammate Conflicts

Not only will you have to handle conflict situations constructively yourself, there will be times when you will need to mediate a conflict that occurs between your teammates. Sometimes the teammates who are in conflict will have the skills and the maturity to resolve it effectively. However, more often than not, they probably won't.

When should you intervene? You need to get involved if the conflict is preventing the individuals from working together effectively on your team. Once the conflict starts showing up on the playing field because people won't communicate with each other or work together, then it is hurting the entire team's chances of success. It would be appropriate for you to intervene if this is the case.

Many conflicts have a tendency to expand beyond the primary people involved as they start to impact and infect everyone on the team. If you see that an issue is spreading to several people on your team, distracting them, or causing them to choose sides, you need to get involved and get everyone refocused.

Encourage your teammates who might be in conflict to use many of the strategies already covered in this chapter. Try to help them clarify the problem, understand each other better, and be open to finding a way to resolve the problem. If for some reason the problem can't be resolved, at least try to get them to agree to disagree and peacefully co-exist with each other on the team. They don't have to like each other but they do have to work together.

Mediator with Teammate and Coach Conflicts

Similarly, you will have to deal with teammates who are frustrated with your coaches. Most of these conflicts will involve a lack of playing time and being frustrated with limited roles. Some teammates will also feel like your coaches are picking on them or that your coaches don't care about them. Whatever the case, if you have earned your teammates' trust, many of them will come to you with their frustrations.

Conflicts between teammates and coaches are tough because you must walk the fine line between understanding how your teammates feel while at the same time respecting your coach's decisions. Your teammates will probably attempt to get you on "their side" by trying to get you to disagree with your coach. Be careful not to fall into that trap. Instead, listen to what they have to say and acknowledge their frustration with the situation. Once they feel you understand them, start getting them to shift their focus to possible solutions. Try to get them to see what they have control over in the situation (controllables vs. uncontrollables). Help them explore possible solutions like talking with the coach about the issue, working harder and having a better attitude, or being patient. You want to help them clarify their thoughts, attempt to look at the situation objectively from all angles, explore possible solutions, and determine the likely consequences of each potential course of action. Assure them you will keep the matter between you, unless they ask you to go to your coach with it.

Athletes Only Meetings

On rare occasions, you may call or find yourself a part of an "Athletes Only" meeting. If you call the meeting, make sure you do it with good reason. Athletes Only meetings should be reserved for very serious situations. It will be your job to lead it and make sure that it is productive. You may need to address specific issues with your teammates and hash out problems. Or you may want to try to get everyone refocused after a series of losses.

A productive way to attempt to solve the problem is an exercise called "Start/ Stop/Continue." Ask your teammates to list their ideas to the following three questions.

1. To get back on track, we need to START . . .

2. To get back on track, we need to STOP. . . .

3. To get back on track, we need to CONTINUE . . .

Collect and discuss your teammates' thoughts on these three questions. Look for similarities and solutions that might work. Then encourage everyone to make a commitment to using the solutions to help the team get back on track.

Your teammates may want to call an Athletes Only meeting to bring up certain issues they are frustrated with and want to see dealt with immediately. As a Vocal Leader, be sure the meeting doesn't turn into a total "Gripe Session." Give people a short window of time to air their concerns. Once the problem has been clearly identified, the rest of the meeting should be focused on possible solutions—not rehashing the problem over and over again.

There are two guidelines you can enforce to help control the meeting and get people focused on the solution. The first is to give your teammates a block of 15 minutes to air their concerns and identify the problem. Once the 15 minutes are up, the rest of the meeting must focus on solutions to the problem. Another way to control the meeting is to allow your teammates to talk about the problems only if they can offer a productive solution to it as well. This gets people to think before they speak instead of reacting and getting caught up in the moment—which is often a challenge in Athletes Only meetings.

Know When to Say When

Using these ideas and strategies, you will probably be able to deal with a lot of situations on your own. However, there are certain situations that can arise which you are not going to be equipped to deal with effectively. These include serious issues like depression, suicide, rape, abuse, eating disorders, etc. Don't ever attempt to deal with these problems on your own. If you sense you are starting to get in over your head, you should encourage the person to get the appropriate help they need. You can even offer to go with them if it would help them feel better. Unfortunately, most teammates will be highly reluctant and even resistant to getting any help.

If you are unsure about how to handle a situation, there should be some professionals around with whom you can talk about the situation anonymously if you would like to protect the person's identity. Talk with someone from your counseling center or your school guidance counselor. These people will know the best ways and resources to get the person the appropriate help they need. Don't go it alone—it's not fair to you or your teammates.

It is also a great idea to keep a small card in your wallet or backpack which lists the contact numbers of people you might need to reach in case of an emergency. You would want to list the work, home, and cell numbers for all of your coaches, trainer, team doctor, and counseling center. Most community's have a crisis hotline number or a help on call number. You might even want to make these cards for everyone on your team to carry with them. Hopefully, you will never need to use these numbers during your career—but you will have them if and when you do.

Finally, if ever someone is in immediate danger of harming themselves or others, try to remove yourself from the situation if possible and call 911 or your local police immediately.

Chapter Ten Summary

Enforcing your team's rules and standards is a difficult yet necessary role you must play as a Vocal Leader. You must be willing to constructively confront your teammates when they get out of line. Use the suggestions in this chapter to help you keep everyone focused and on track. You won't always be liked by your teammates, but you will earn their respect.

WEEK 10

KEY POINTS FROM CHAPTER TEN

List three to five major points or insights you gained from this chapter:

1. _____
2. _____
3. _____
4. _____
5. _____

PRACTICAL EXERCISES FOR CHAPTER TEN

1. Interview someone who deals with conflict on a regular basis (mediator, customer service representative, judge, attorney) Ask them:

- What are the toughest challenges of your job?

_____

_____

- What conflict styles do you observe others using?

_____

_____

- What style(s) do you tend to use in conflict situations?

_____

_____

- What advice do you have for me when it comes to addressing conflict?

_____

_____

2. Develop a relationship with some helping professionals whom you could turn to if someone on your team ever faces a serious crisis (guidance counselor, counselors at the counseling center/student health, etc.). Introduce yourself to these people and find out more about them and the kinds of services they can provide. Take back any brochures or tip sheets they might have and make them available in the locker room.

COACH/CAPTAIN MEETING NOTES

WEEK 10

Next Meeting Date:
Time:

SUMMARY

"It's what you learn after you know it all that counts."
JOHN WOODEN, LEGENDARY UCLA MEN'S BASKETBALL COACH

As you come to the end of this manual, I'd like to try to encapsulate everything we covered into what I call the Seven "R's" of Being a Respected Team Leader.

The Seven "R's" of Respected Team Leaders

1. Role Model
All leadership begins with self leadership. People will come to respect you only if you can walk your own talk and lead yourself effectively. You must be able to model the commitment, confidence, composure, and character you expect from your teammates.

2. Remind
As a team leader, you must continually remind your teammates about what is important—your common goal, your game plan, and your team chemistry. Remind your teammates that all of the commitments and sacrifices they are making will pay off in the end.

3. Reinforce
You'll also spend a lot of time reinforcing the positive strides your teammates make. Be sure to compliment them often as a way to build their confidence and fuel a positive momentum and environment on your team.

4. Re-energize
There will be many times during practices and competition when you will need to pick up the energy level and enthusiasm of your teammates. As a leader, provide a spark of inspiration to turn a passive team into a passionate team.

5. Reassure

Because there are so many obstacles, setbacks, and adversities involved in every season, you will need to reassure your teammates when they are feeling nervous, scared, frustrated, helpless, and hopeless. Give them a sense of hope and optimism.

6. Refocus

You will spend a lot of time helping your teammates refocus their negative thoughts on something more positive and productive. Shift their minds from the distractions and problems to workable solutions.

7. Reprimand

Last but not least, you must have the ability to constructively confront and reprimand your teammates when necessary. You must hold them accountable to live up to and maintain your team's rules and standards.

Team Captain's Weekly Monitoring Sheet

Although the information in the manual is coming to an end, you will need to continually monitor yourself and your team. The Captain's Weekly Monitoring Sheet is designed to help you evaluate your leadership skills and keep tabs on your team throughout your season. I encourage you to find a specific time each week to reflect on the questions and fill out your responses. I also advise you to maintain regular contact with your coach, either with continued weekly meetings or informal chats. You can use the information from the weekly sheet as you and your coach keep your team on track.

Ongoing Evaluation

You'll also see that I have included another copy of the Team Leader Self Evaluation. After spending the last 10 weeks examining the topic of leadership and improving your skills, take a few minutes to evaluate yourself again. I hope that you find some areas where you have improved as well as some areas that still will require your attention. Continue evaluating yourself from time to time throughout the season and your career. I would also encourage you to have your coach and teammates evaluate you as well.

COMPANION ONLINE LEADERSHIP RESOURCE

**For more information,
visit www.TeamCaptainsNetwork.com**

Captain's Weekly Monitoring Sheet

Using a 1 (terrible) to 10 (great) scale, how would I rate myself as a leader this past week on each of the six key components of leadership?

Date:

Self Leadership

How would I rate myself as a leader this past week on a 1 (terrible) to 10 (great) scale?

_____ _____ _____ _____ _____ _____

Commitment, Confidence, Composure, Character, Encourager, Enforcer

What went well? (highlights)

_____

_____

What didn't go so well? (concerns)

_____

_____

What might I do differently next time? (lessons)

_____

_____

Team Leadership

What is the mood of our team right now?

distracted	1	2	3	4	5	6	7	8	9	10	focused
conflicted	1	2	3	4	5	6	7	8	9	10	confident
passive	1	2	3	4	5	6	7	8	9	10	aggressive
conflicted	1	2	3	4	5	6	7	8	9	10	unified
fatigued	1	2	3	4	5	6	7	8	9	10	fresh
apathetic	1	2	3	4	5	6	7	8	9	10	motivated
frustrated	1	2	3	4	5	6	7	8	9	10	having fun

Who is struggling right now—how might I reach out to them?

_____

_____

Is there anything I need to prepare for/guard against this coming week?

_____

_____

Observations/Comments:

_____

_____

TEAM LEADERSHIP SELF EVALUATION

Using a scale from one to five rate yourself on the following 24 questions.

1 = Strongly Disagree, 2 = Disagree, 3 = Undecided, 4 = Agree, 5 = Strongly Agree

	SD	D	U	A	SA

Commitment
1. I am one of the hardest workers on the team 1 2 3 4 5
2. I care passionately about the team's success.................................... 1 2 3 4 5
3. I am a competitive person who wants to win... 1 2 3 4 5

Confidence
4. I believe in myself as a person and my ability to lead 1 2 3 4 5
5. I want to perform in pressure situations 1 2 3 4 5
6. I bounce back quickly following mistakes and errors 1 2 3 4 5

Composure
7. I stay calm and composed in pressure situations 1 2 3 4 5
8. I stay focused when faced with distractions, obstacles, and adversity..... 1 2 3 4 5
9. I keep my anger and frustration under control 1 2 3 4 5

Character
10. I consistently do the right thing on and off the court/field....................... 1 2 3 4 5
11. I am honest and trustworthy... 1 2 3 4 5
12. I treat my teammates, coaches, and others with respect....................... 1 2 3 4 5

LEADER BY EXAMPLE TOTAL (add questions 1–12)

Encourager—Servant
13. I reach out to teammates when they need help 1 2 3 4 5
14. I take the time to listen to my teammates 1 2 3 4 5

Encourager—Confidence Builder
15. I regularly encourage my teammates to do their best........................... 1 2 3 4 5
16. I regularly compliment my teammates when they succeed 1 2 3 4 5

Encourager—Refocuser
17. I communicate optimism and hope when the team is struggling 1 2 3 4 5
18. I know what to say to my teammates when they are struggling............. 1 2 3 4 5

Encourager—Team Builder
19. I have developed an effective relationship with each of my teammates. 1 2 3 4 5
20. I am a team player who seeks to unify the team................................... 1 2 3 4 5

Enforcer
21. I hold my teammates accountable for following team rules/standards... 1 2 3 4 5
22. I constructively confront my teammates when necessary...................... 1 2 3 4 5
23. I am willing to address and minimize conflicts between teammates...... 1 2 3 4 5
24. I am firm, fair, and direct when dealing with conflicts and problems 1 2 3 4 5

VOCAL LEADER TOTAL (add questions 1–24)

MAKE A REAL DIFFERENCE

I'd also like to take this opportunity to remind you to use your leadership skills to make a real difference outside of your sport too. Your school and community desperately need responsible and respected leaders like yourself. There are hundreds of children who need positive role models, someone to read to them, and someone to care. There are people your age who need your support and encouragement as they try to figure out who they are and what is important to them. And there are numerous adults who have sold themselves short and have given up on life. Let your passion, enthusiasm, and compassion offer them a sense of hope. Be sure to do your part. The world needs you.

———————————————————————

"Never doubt that a small group of thoughtful, committed people can change the world. Indeed, it is the only thing that ever has."
MARGARET MEAD

Here are two of my favorite quotes that reflect the enormous responsibility and potential you have as a leader. My hope is that these quotes inspire you to make a real difference.

The Paradoxical Commandments

People are illogical, unreasonable, and self-centered.

Love them anyway.

If you do good, people will accuse you of selfish ulterior motives.

Do good anyway.

If you are successful, you win false friends and true enemies.

Succeed anyway.

The good you do today will be forgotten tomorrow.

Do good anyway.

Honesty and frankness make you vulnerable.

Be honest and frank anyway.

The biggest men and women with the biggest ideas can be shot down by the smallest men and women with the smallest minds.

Think big anyway.

People favor underdogs but follow only top dogs.

Fight for a few underdogs anyway.

What you spend years building may be destroyed overnight.

Build anyway.

People really need help but may attack you if you do help them.

Help people anyway.

Give the world the best you have and you'll get kicked in the teeth.

Give the world the best you have anyway.

Dr. Kent M. Keith

"This is the true joy in life, the being used for a purpose recognized by yourself as a mighty one; being a force of nature instead of the feverish little clod of ailments and grievances complaining that the world will not devote itself to making you happy.

I am of the opinion that my life belongs to the whole community and as long as I live, it is my privilege to do for it whatever I can.

I want to be thoroughly used up when I die, for the harder I work the more I live.

I rejoice in life for its own sake.

Life is no brief candle to me. It is a sort of splendid torch which I have got a hold of for the moment, and I want to make it burn as brightly as possible before handing it on to future generations."

George Bernard Shaw

PLEASE SHARE YOUR FEEDBACK WITH ME

Finally, thank you for the privilege of sharing your leadership journey with you! I sincerely hope that the strategies, stories, exercises, experiences, and discussions you had throughout the course of this manual inspired and challenged you to become a better leader.

I strongly encourage you to contact me to share any feedback you might have after completing this manual. Let me know what you liked, didn't like, what's missing, and what could be improved. I am continually updating this manual and looking to incorporate new and better ideas, exercises, and activities. Feel free to share any of your personal stories as you continue your leadership journey. Your comments will make a difference for future leaders who will read the manual. Please e-mail me at jeff@jeffjanssen.com—I look forward to hearing from you!

CONTINUE YOUR LEADERSHIP JOURNEY WITH THE ADVANCED TEAM CAPTAIN'S CULTURE MANUAL

Now that you have learned how to effectively lead yourself and your teammates, you are ready to take your leadership to a higher and deeper level by learning how to lead your entire team. The advanced *Team Captain's Culture Manual* is the next level of leadership training and shows you how to lead your team by building a positive and productive culture.

Along with your fellow leaders and coaches, the *Team Captain's Culture Manual* teaches you what it takes to build and sustain a Championship Culture in your program. And, like the *Team Captain's Leadership Manual* you just completed, the advanced *Culture Manual* is written in a bite-sized, 10-module workbook format complete with evaluations, checklists, exercises, and captain and coach meeting notes to help you effectively assess and improve your team's culture.

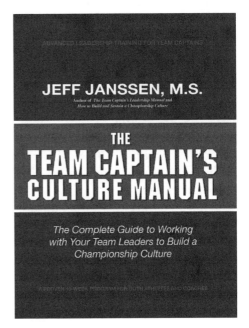

The advanced *Team Captain's Culture Manual* teaches you:
- The 8 Kinds of Cultures and which one is best for your team
- The 6 Key Components of a Championship Culture
- How to develop a Clear and Compelling Vision that truly inspires your team
- How to establish and enforce high Standards of Behavior for your team
- A Proven 10-Step Blueprint to Build a Championship Culture in Your Program

---

"I've been in the business 30 years and there are a lot of different programs I've seen. The Janssen Sports Leadership Center's programs and resources are the best out there. The programming builds on itself and is not just a one-time seminar. You will see a change in student-athletes in terms of leadership on the field, in the classroom, and everywhere else."

JEFF LONG, ARKANSAS DIRECTOR OF ATHLETICS,
COLLEGE FOOTBALL SELECTION COMMITTEE CHAIRMAN

To learn more about the advanced *Team Captain's Culture Manual*, visit
www.janssensportsleadership.com/resources/team-captains-culture-manual/

ABOUT THE AUTHOR

Widely considered the world's top expert on Sports Leadership, Jeff Janssen is the founder and president of the Janssen Sports Leadership Center.

Jeff and his top-notch team's pioneering work on sports leadership development with student-athletes and coaches has led to the creation of cutting edge Leadership Academies at North Carolina, Illinois, Arkansas, Colorado, Michigan, LSU, NC State, Notre Dame, Pitt, Yale, Georgetown, Stanford, Wake Forest, Baylor, Houston, UNC-Charlotte, Colgate, Lafayette, Holy Cross, George Washington, Colby, Fordham, St. Francis Xavier, Guelph, Winston-Salem State, Boston University, Loyola, and Lehigh.

A prolific author, he has authored numerous books including *The Team Captain's Leadership Manual, How to Build and Sustain a Championship Culture, Championship Team Building, The Commitment Continuum™ System, Jeff Janssen's Peak Performance Playbook, How to Develop Relentless Competitors, Develop Relentless Competitors Drillbook,* and *The Seven Secrets of Successful Coaches.*

Jeff also is the co-founder of Student-Athletes Leading Social Change (SALSC). SALSC's mission is to catalyze and connect current and former college student-athletes who want to use the leadership skills to change the world. The organization has raised over $200,000 to build or refurbish schools for impoverished communities in Kenya, Ecuador, Chicago, New Orleans, Philadelphia, and Washington, D.C.

Jeff and his family live in Cary, North Carolina and enjoy playing and watching sports, traveling, and reading.

www.JanssenSportsLeadership.com

www.salsc.org

JANSSEN SPORTS LEADERSHIP CENTER PROGRAMS

LEADERSHIP SUMMIT

Our highly engaging and interactive Leadership Summit teaches your athletes the sports leadership skills and strategies necessary to be strong and effective leaders for your team. Based on our world-famous Sports Leadership Academies at top colleges across the nation, your student-athletes can learn some of the same sports leadership skills taught at high-level programs.

The 75-minute Leadership Summit is an interactive workshop designed for emerging and existing student-athlete leaders at the college, high school, or club level. The program also includes a dedicated 75-minute workshop for coaches on how best to develop, select, and partner with your leaders.

LEADERSHIP RETREAT

The more intensive Leadership Retreat includes up to six hours of advanced leadership training for student-athletes and coaches conducted in a fun and fast-paced environment. The programming targets two separate student-athlete groups, Emerging Leaders and Veteran Leaders, based on their readiness to assume leadership roles. We also provide an advanced leadership workshop for the coaching staff.

Plus, to reinforce and extend the programming throughout the year, the participants also receive a copy of *The Team Captain's Leadership Manual* and a year-long membership to the TeamCaptainsNetwok.com. The Leadership Retreat makes a great early season option to provide your leaders with the knowledge and skills they'll need to step up and lead throughout the season.

LEADERSHIP ACADEMY

The comprehensive Leadership Academy provides your athletic department with an ongoing and integrated approach to leadership development. We target and train three distinct groups of leaders (Emerging Leaders, Veteran Leaders, Leadership 360) and distribute the training with multiple modules offered throughout the school year to maximize learning, retention, and application.

In addition to the programming, the Leadership Academy also includes educational resources for all participants to reinforce and extend the learning as well as an ongoing consulting retainer with the Janssen Sports Leadership Center for advice and troubleshooting various issues that arise throughout the year.

For more info on the Janssen Sports Leadership Center visit

www.JanssenSportsLeadership.com

WHAT TOP ADs AND COACHES ARE SAYING...

"I've been in the business 30 years and there are a lot of different programs I've seen. What the Janssen Sports Leadership Center does is the best out there. It builds on itself. It is not a one-time seminar. You will see a change in student-athletes in terms of leadership on the field, in the classroom, and everywhere else."

Jeff Long, *Arkansas Athletics Director*

"Jeff Janssen's work with our student-athletes through the Michigan Leadership Academy has been tremendous. His ability to communicate with our student-athletes, along with his ability to draw student-athletes into deeper discussions about leadership is outstanding. We are fortunate to work with Jeff and experience firsthand the way he gives student-athletes insight into how they think, how they perceive, how they process, and how they can become great teammates and performers."

John Beilein, *Michigan Men's Basketball Coach*

"I have great admiration and respect for Jeff Janssen's work with coaches and student-athletes. His innovative ideas have made a difference in our program as well as many programs across the country. He has the unique ability to transform critical concepts like leadership, team building, and mental toughness into practical and easy to use strategies that can be implemented by coaches and athletes alike."

Pat Summitt, *Former Tennessee Women's Basketball Coach*

"The Carolina Leadership Academy is one of the finest things our athletic department has done in the over thirty years I have been here. I can clearly see the program's impact on and off the field."

Anson Dorrance, *North Carolina Women's Soccer Coach*

"Jeff is an amazing motivator and a truly great listener. He challenged the student-athletes at the University of Illinois to become greater than they imagined, not just in their sport, but in life. He also encouraged us to give back to our local community and to be the selfless and courageous leaders that would impact our university, community, country, and the world. Jeff's passion and commitment to the Leadership Academy is indomitable. He has had an immeasurable impact on so many student-athletes lives. He's given many of us the confidence to succeed, the willingness to do more, and the commitment needed for life."

CeCe Marizu, *Former Illinois Women's Swimmer*

For more info on the Janssen Sports Leadership Center visit

www.JanssenSportsLeadership.com

NOTES

Coaches' Introduction and Overview

xii Mike Krzyzewski: Billy Packer and Roland Lazenby, *Why We Win* (1999), p. 206.
xii Interview with Kay Yow.
xiii Rick Pitino and Bill Reynolds, *Lead to Succeed* (2000), p. 43.
xiii Interview with Mike Candrea.
xiii Chuck Noll: Billy Packer and Roland Lazenby, *Why We Win* (1999).
xiii Interview with Jerry Yeagley.
xvi Mike Krzyzewski and Donald T. Phillips, *Leading with the Heart* (2000), p. 273.
xxiv John C. Maxwell, *The 21 Irrefutable Laws of Leadership* (1998), p. 212.

Athletes' Introduction and Overview

xxxi Mike Krzyzewski: Billy Packer and Roland Lazenby, *Why We Win* (1999), p. 206.
xxxi Interview with Kay Yow.
xxxii Rick Pitino and Bill Reynolds, *Lead to Succeed* (2000), p. 43.
xxxii Interview with Mike Candrea.
xxxii Chuck Noll: Billy Packer and Roland Lazenby, *Why We Win* (1999).
xxxii Interview with Jerry Yeagley.
xxxiv Vince Lombardi: *Joe Montana's Art and Magic of Quarterbacking* (1997), p. 93.
xxxv Lauren Gregg and Tim Nash, *The Champion Within* (1999), p. 255.

Chapter One

1 James MacGregor Burns, *Leadership* (1978).
2 Peter Drucker: Jack Beatty, *The World According to Peter Drucker* (1998).
2 Warren Bennis, *On Becoming a Leader* (1989).
2 John C. Maxwell, *Developing the Leader Within You* (1993).
3 Joe Torre and Henry Dreher, *Joe Torre's Ground Rules for Winners* (1999), p. 270.
5 Joe Montana, *Joe Montana's Art and Magic of Quarterbacking* (1997), p. 10.
5 Rick Pitino and Bill Reynolds, *Lead to Succeed* (2000), p. 198.
6 Larry Bird, *Bird Watching* (2000).
6 Michael Jordan, *I Can't Accept Not Trying* (1994), p. 34.
9 Phil Jackson, *Sacred Hoops* (1995).
12 Michael Jordan, *I Can't Accept Not Trying* (1994), p. 32.
12 Jason Giambi: Baseball's Leading Men, *Baseball America* (Vol. XI, No. 37), p. 9.
19 Joe Montana, *Joe Montana's Art and Magic of Quarterbacking* (1997), p. 99.
19 Bobby Bowden and Steve Bowden, *The Bowden Way* (2001), p. 244.

Chapter Two

28 Joe Namath: Michael Lynberg, *Winning* (1993).
29 Jim Kouzes and Barry Posner, *Encouraging the Heart* (2002), p. 143.
33 Michael Jordan, *I Can't Accept Not Trying* (1994), p. 32.

33 Joe Montana, *Joe Montana's Art and Magic of Quarterbacking* (1997), p. 97.
34 Merlin Olsen: Michael Lynberg, *Winning* (1993).
34 Jeff Bagwell: Baseball's Leading Men, *Baseball America* (Vol. XI, No. 37), p. 12.
34 Jason Giambi: Baseball's Leading Men, *Baseball America* (Vol. XI, No. 37), p. 8.

Chapter Three—Confidence

39 Interview with Pat Summitt.
41 Brett Favre and Chris Havel, *Favre* (1997).
45 Martin Seligman, *Learned Optimism* (1991).

Chapter Four—Composure

51 Joe Montana, *Joe Montana's Art and Magic of Quarterbacking* (1997), p. 97.
52 Mike Krzyzewski and Donald T. Phillips, *Leading with the Heart* (2000).
52 Ken Ravizza and Tom Hanson, *Heads Up Baseball* (1995).

Chapter Five—Character

63 Norman Schwarzkopf: Robert Pater, *Leading from Within* (1999), p. 10.
64 Interview with Rhonda Revelle.
68 Gary Barnett and Vahe Gregorian, *High Hopes* (1996).

Section Two

73 Lauren Gregg and Tim Nash, *The Champion Within* (1999), p. 260.

Chapter Six—Servant Leader

79 Magic Johnson: Michael Lynberg, *Winning* (1993).
81 Robert Greenleaf, *Servant Leadership* (1977).
81 Don Mattingly: Don Meyer handout.
82 Brett Favre and Chris Havel, *Favre* (1997).
83 Jason Giambi: Baseball's Leading Men, *Baseball America* (Vol. XI, No. 37), p. 8.

Chapter Seven—Confidence-Builder

89 Interview with Marty Schottenheimer.
90 Jason Giambi: Baseball's Leading Men, *Baseball America* (Vol. XI, No. 37), p. 10.
90 Mike Krzyzewski and Donald T. Phillips, *Leading with the Heart* (2000), p. 26.
93 Rick Pitino and Bill Reynolds, *Lead to Succeed* (2000), p. 40.
95 Dawn Staley: Kim Doren and Charlie Jones, *If Winning Were Easy, Everyone Would   Do It* (2002).
95 Carla Overbeck: Lauren Gregg and Tim Nash, *The Champion Within* (1999), p. 260.

Chapter Eight—Refocuser

99 Rick Pitino and Bill Reynolds, *Lead to Succeed* (2000), p. 42.
99 Mike Krzyzewski and Donald T. Phillips, *Leading with the Heart* (2000), p. 157.
100 Julie Foudy: Lauren Gregg and Tim Nash, *The Champion Within* (1999), p. 260.
102 Joe Torre and Henry Dreher, *Joe Torre's Ground Rules for Winners* (1999).
102 Bobby Bowden and Steve Bowden, *The Bowden Way* (2001), p. 31.

Chapter Nine—Team Builder

111 Pat Williams, *The Magic of Teamwork* (1997).

115 Scottie Pippen: Michael Lynberg, *Winning* (1993).

115 Rick Pitino and Bill Reynolds, *Lead to Succeed* (2000), p. 51.

116 Julie Foudy: Lauren Gregg and Tim Nash, *The Champion Within* (1999), p. 257.

Chapter Ten—Enforcer

123 Pat Summitt and Sally Jenkins, *Reach for the Summitt* (1998), p. 97.

125 Joe Montana, *Joe Montana's Art and Magic of Quarterbacking* (1997), p. 97.

125 Mike Krzyzewski and Donald T. Phillips, *Leading with the Heart* (2000), p. 84.

126 Joe Montana, *Joe Montana's Art and Magic of Quarterbacking* (1997), p. 106.

127 David Johnson, *Reaching Out* (1993).

132 J.S. Greenberg, *Coping with Stress* (1990).

Summary

144 Kent M. Keith, *Anyway* (2001).

Photo Credits

Table of Contents—Marcus Ginyard courtesy of University of North Carolina Media Relations.

Coaches' Introduction—Coach Mike Krzyzewski courtesy of Duke University Photography, Mike Candrea courtesy of University of Arizona Media Relations.

Athletes' Introduction—Arizona men's basketball team courtesy of University of Arizona Media Relations, Jenny Mainz courtesy of University of Florida Media Relations, Beau DeBruin courtesy of Little Chute High School, North Carolina Women's Soccer Team courtesy of University of North Carolina Media Relations.

Section 1—Jeremy Stultz courtesy of Pitt Media Relations and Penny Semaia.

Chapter 1—Jennie Finch courtesy of Mizuno and USA Softball.

Chapter 2—Kirk Urso courtesy of University of North Carolina Media Relations.

Chapter 3—Jaime Pisani courtesy of University of Arkansas Media Relations.

Page 48—Jessica Hootz courtesy of Colgate Media Relations.

Chapter 4—J Lehman courtesy of University of Illinois Media Relations.

Chapter 5— Juliana Stern courtesy of George Washington Media Relations.

Section 2—Hillary Haen courtesy of University of Illinois Media Relations.

Page 77—D.J. Baxendale courtesy of University of Arkansas Media Relations.

Chapter 6—Kara Cannizzaro courtesy of University of North Carolina Media Relations.

Chapter 7—Tim Hardaway and Trey Burke courtesy of University of North Carolina Media Relations.

Chapter 8—Lindsay Tarpley courtesy of University of North Carolina Media Relations.

Chapter 9—Central Missouri State Baseball Team courtesy of Central Missouri State University Athletics Media Relations.

Page 120—Liz Lucas courtesy of Lehigh Media Relations.

Chapter 10—Jeanne Kenney courtesy of Tony Beaulieu.

Summary—Sabatino Chen courtesy of University of Colorado Media Relations, Sarah Frohnapfel courtesy of Lafayette Media Relations, Shawn Hunwick courtesy of University of Michigan Media Relations, Ashley Walsh courtesy of Colgate Media Relations.

INDEX

JANSSEN SPORTS LEADERSHIP CENTER RESOURCES

THE TEAM CAPTAIN'S CULTURE MANUAL (book)
This advanced leadership training program shows coaches and captains how to work together to build a winning culture. Includes a 10-week Championship Culture building program to help your leaders create a positive and productive culture in your program. $29.95

HOW TO BUILD AND SUSTAIN A CHAMPIONSHIP CULTURE (book)
Written for coaches and athletic directors, this book reveals the 6 Key Components that all Championship Cultures have in common. Includes a 10-Step Culture Building Blueprint. $29.95

THE COMMITMENT CONTINUUM™ SYSTEM (book)
This six-week Commitment Training System teaches your athletes what it means to make a serious and total commitment to their task, training, and team. Apply the system to develop highly Committed and Compelled athletes and teams. Packages available in 10, 20, and 100.

CHAMPIONSHIP TEAM BUILDING (book)
This groundbreaking book details dozens of proven strategies to help you develop great team chemistry. discover the Seven "C's" of Championship Team Building. Solve the problems that could distract, divide, and destroy your team. Includes 38 team building drills. $29.95

THE SEVEN SECRETS OF SUCCESSFUL COACHES (book)
Learn how to get the absolute most out of your players using the coaching strategies of sport's most successful coaches including Pat Summitt, Mike Krzyzewski, Mike Candrea, and many others. Discover how to create confident, consistent, and coachable athletes. $29.95

HOW TO DEVELOP RELENTLESS COMPETITORS (book)
Looking to transform your passive, wimpy, and entitled athletes into focused and fierce Competitors? learn the inside strategies that sport's top coaches use to train and develop their athletes into relentless Competitors. $29.95

For more info on the Janssen Sports Leadership Center visit

www.JanssenSportsLeadership.com